The Interim Pastor's Manual

The Interim
Pastor's Manual

Alan G. Gripe

The Geneva Press
Philadelphia

Book design by Gene Harris

First edition

Published by The Geneva Press®
Philadelphia, Pennsylvania

PRINTED IN THE UNITED STATES OF AMERICA

9 8 7 6 5 4 3 2 1

Library of Congress Catalog Card No. 87-10733
ISBN 0–664–24090–9

Contents

Introduction

This manual was originally developed for the Joint Task Force on a More Effective Placement System of the Presbyterian Church in the United States and The United Presbyterian Church in the U.S.A. It is designed for four audiences: the Interim Pastor, the Session, the Congregation, and the Presbytery Committee on Ministry. Others who are likely to find it useful are members of Presbytery or Synod staffs whose tasks relate to the leadership of congregations. Some sections deal with matters of more concern to one of these audiences than to the others. It will be beneficial, however, for each group to understand all the aspects involved in interim service.

Churches exploring whether or not to seek an Interim Pastor will be especially interested in chapters 1, 3 (third section), 4, and 6. Churches negotiating with an Interim Pastor will also want to give special attention to chapter 5 and Appendixes A and B. Persons interested in becoming Interim Pastors may want to begin reading chapters 1, 3, 4, and 7. The Committee on Ministry will want to be familiar with the entire manual. (For convenience, we refer to this committee throughout by the abbreviation COM.)

A variety of special resources, ideas, examples, and models are included. Except for the quotations from the Presbyterian *Book of Order,* the entire manual is to be understood only as advice and counsel, and each presbytery is free to establish its own policies and procedures. Relevant passages from the *Book of Order* are quoted in the opening pages of chapter 1, but readers are reminded that the Interim Pastors movement is in a developmental stage and there may be relevant changes in the *Book of Order* at any General Assembly. *Congregations, sessions, and ministers should remember that specific guidance from presbytery will always supersede any advice in this manual.*

It is desirable for each presbytery to approve formally a Presbytery Policy and Procedure paper to guide COM, sessions, and Interim Pastors. We hope this manual will be helpful in preparing such a policy statement.

Advocacy for the wide use of Interim Pastors and a desire to recruit more and better qualified persons to undertake this type of service as a form of specialized ministry are additional reasons why this manual has been prepared. Presbyteries and synods themselves need to recognize why interim ministries are of critical importance to our church today. Further, middle governing bodies need to have data available in concise and persuasive form to present to sessions the reasons for employing qualified Interim Pastors when there is need for short-term pastoral leadership for the congregation.

Pastors themselves need to understand both the opportunity and the challenge in serving as *intentional* Interim Pastors. More qualified persons of all ages are needed right now who are willing to polish those special skills required for this particular ministry. Above all, recognition needs to be given to those pioneers in this field whose devotion to the church has inspired them to endure the risks and hardships that interim service sometimes imposes.

Many persons have shared in the development of this manual. Several doctoral dissertations, conference reports, occasional papers, and studies by pastors and church executives have served as background in its preparation. Numbers of church leaders, both laity and clergy, have read each of the first three drafts and made many helpful suggestions.

The Vocation Agency and the Office of Professional Development wish to thank all whose participation made this manual possible. Mary V. Atkinson was especially helpful in making sure the manual reflects an appreciation for the policies and traditions of the Presbyterian Church in the United States. She also assisted in editing several drafts of it and in the development and leadership of the Interim Pastors Seminars at Montreat and Ghost Ranch, where a great deal has been learned about the interim experience in the parish church. Particular gratitude goes to Ray Heer, who prepared much of the first draft; to Edward Huenemann, Margaret Morris, and others who contributed to the section on theology; and to Robert Buxbaum, Frederick Christian, Raymond Kent, Joan Mabon, James Memmott, Lawrence Spencer, and Joyce Stedge, all experienced interim ministers whose papers, thinking, and sharing have made this a more useful statement than it would otherwise have been. We also acknowledge with much appreciation the helpful suggestions of those pastors, elders, and church executives and many spouses of Interim Pastors and church executives who have been students and teachers in the seminars at Ghost Ranch and Montreat for several years, a wonderful list far too long to be included here. We express sincere thanks to Anne Walline, Felicity Langford, and Prudence Welsh, all of whom meticulously typed many drafts of the manuscript and assisted in numerous other ways to make this manual possible.

Alan G. Gripe, Coordinator
Committees on Ministry
The Vocation Agency

1

The Meaning of Interim: A Time and a Person

An Interim Pastor is one who temporarily assumes the leadership of a congregation that is without an installed pastor while a Pastor Nominating Committee is at work, or of a congregation where the Committee on Ministry (COM) expects that a Pastor Nominating Committee will soon be elected. The term "interim" means this person serves for a limited period of time *between* two installed pastors while the congregation, through its elected nominating committee, is conducting its search. This interim person is called "pastor" because the work covers most or all tasks of an installed pastor plus special tasks that are needed only during the interval between installed pastors. These tasks include grief work, preparation for change in the ministry and mission, and preparing the congregation to accept a new installed pastor. Successful completion of these assignments generally requires the experience, skill, and focus of intention that qualify interim pastoral service to be considered a form of specialized ministry.

Many congregations, presbyteries, and synods are now using Interim Pastors in a variety of ways. Some serve as head of staff and others as solo pastors or as associates, the majority being in one of those first two positions. A Pastor Nominating Committee may take a few weeks longer to find a pastor when there is an Interim serving the congregation, but the result generally is a better match between the installed pastor and the church. Equally important, such congregations are usually better prepared to receive a new pastor after having had an Interim, particularly if the Interim Pastor, Pastor Nominating Committee, and COM are all doing their jobs well. This means longer, more satisfying pastorates and therefore fewer pastoral changes because of dissatisfaction with the pastor, the congregation, or the session.

The term "interim" is also sometimes used to describe specialized consultants who are called to serve a congregation for a limited time to perform a specific assignment; for example, to conduct a survey of the congregation or community, to solve a problem, to assist in goal-setting for redevelopment, to resolve a conflict, or to meet some other specific need that present church leaders are not equipped to handle.

Interim specialists are also being employed today in executive positions in all the governing bodies beyond the congregation; that is, in presbyteries, synods, and the General Assembly. In addition, a variety of church-related institutions such as hospitals, schools, and colleges make use of interim professional personnel when the need arises. A term that covers all such forms of interim service today is "Interim Ministry Specialist." What follows in this manual is aimed primarily at the pastor serving a session and a congregation, but other interim specialists should find the information and guidance offered here to be genuinely worthwhile whatever type of interim assignment may engage them.

The "In-Between" Time

When the pastoral or other major staff position becomes vacant, it not only occasions a sense of loss on the part of the congregation, leading them to look to the past, but also provides an opportunity to look forward. It is a time when a constructive ministry is possible, one that can have lasting benefits. It is an excellent time for renewal.

Steps in Changing Pastoral Leadership

In *Changing Pastoral Leadership,* Loren Mead, Director of the Alban Institute in Washington, D.C., has recorded seven steps involved in the process.

1. The period of termination: when the former pastor is still on site after announcement of the decision to leave
2. The period of direction-finding: when the congregation (or session) finds out what to do, what committees to appoint, and what sources of help it wants to ask for
3. The period of self-study: when the congregation looks at itself to see who it is, who it wants to be, and consequently what kind of leadership it needs

4. The period of search: when the congregation searches the field to find the pastor they want to call

5. The period of negotiation and decision: when the search narrows down to a single candidate, decisions are made, and agreements negotiated

6. The period of installation: when the new pastor arrives and gets installed in office, officially and unofficially

7. The period of start-up: when pastor and people get their work going, explore each other's expectations, and define each other's roles and relationships

Mead notes that this outline may be misleading if it is too rigidly applied, but it is a useful frame of reference.

Stages in the Congregation's Feeling Responses

As the foregoing steps are taking place, it is important to note the various feelings that are usually being experienced by the congregation.

1. Relief or anger over the pastor's leaving
2. Guilt over some aspects of the past
3. Insecurity about the present and the future
4. Recognition of the reality of the situation
5. Awareness of the need for some help
6. Hope for the future
7. Excitement about a new pastor

Understanding and responding supportively to such feelings is a significant part of the interim leader's task, a task that is complicated by the fact that these feelings are experienced at different times and in different ways by various members of the congregation. Further, there is seldom a neat or steady progression from one step to another, whether one considers groups or individuals. The goal is, at last, to bring everyone in the congregation (or as many as possible) to the final step, excitement about the new pastor. The person who can do this truly deserves to be called "specialist."

Interim Leadership

Whenever a vacancy occurs, the presbytery COM extends its care to the congregation by counseling with the session concerning the kinds of temporary pastoral services available during the interim time. Before examining interim ministry in detail, let us look at the other options provided in the *Book of Order.*

Varieties of Options

There are three categories in Presbyterian tradition under which ministers may temporarily serve a church that is without a regular pastor: the Occasional or Temporary Supply, the Stated Supply, and the newest category, the Interim Supply, also known as Interim Pastor. It is unwise to assume automatically that choosing the interim category is best for most congregations while they are seeking a new pastor. The COM should lead the session in a study of all three categories before any decision is made.

The *Book of Order* describes these temporary ministries in Section G-14.0513 as follows:

> When a church does not have a pastor, or while the pastor is unable to perform her or his duties, the session should obtain the services of a minister of this denomination in a temporary pastoral relation. Temporary pastoral relations are those of stated supply, interim supply, or temporary supply:
>
> a. A stated supply is a minister appointed by the presbytery, after consultation with the session, to perform the functions of a pastor in a church. The relation shall be established only by the presbytery and shall extend for a period not to exceed twelve months at a time. A stated supply shall not be reappointed until the presbytery, through its committee on ministry, has reviewed her or his effectiveness. No formal call shall be issued by the congregation and no formal installation shall take place. A stated supply who is a member of the presbytery may, with presbytery's approval, serve as moderator of the session.
>
> b. An interim supply is a minister invited by the session to preach the Word, administer the Sacraments, and fulfill pastoral duties for a specified period not to exceed twelve months at a time, while the church is seeking a pastor. The session may not secure an interim supply without seeking the counsel of presbytery through its committee on ministry. A minister may not be called to be a pastor or associate pastor of a church served as interim supply, unless six months have elapsed since the end of the temporary relationship.
>
> c. A temporary supply may be a minister, a candidate, a commissioned lay preacher, or an elder secured by the session to conduct services when the pastor is unable to perform pastoral duties. The session shall seek the counsel of presbytery through its committee on ministry before securing a temporary supply.

Choosing the Right Option

The presbytery's Committee on Ministry should study all three options carefully to familiarize themselves with each one so that when needs arise it will be possible to determine accurately which would be of the most service in each case.

Temporary Supply. A Temporary Supply is normally approved when the services rendered are limited in time or scope. Exceptions are usually by recommendation of COM or the mission planning committee of presbytery.

Stated Supply. A Stated Supply is normally approved:

1. When the congregation is not prepared to work through the customary search process, resulting in an expectation of a longer interim period.

2. When the congregation, COM, and presbytery committee responsible for mission planning all agree that full use of the usual search process would not be appropriate or helpful; for example, when there is no expectation that the congregation can call a new pastor or when on a long-term basis a congregation can only afford part-time staff who are not to be installed.

3. When filling the pastoral vacancy involves arrangements with personnel or churches of other denominations.

A Stated Supply can be called as the installed pastor of the congregation that he or she has been serving by a vote of the congregation and by a majority vote of the presbytery. Such steps should not be taken, however, without a careful consultation with COM. Neither COM nor the presbytery itself should ever allow this action to circumvent presbytery's Equal Employment Opportunity policies.

Initiative for establishing the Stated Supply position generally lies with the presbytery, although a session may share the initiative with presbytery under some circumstances. If there is serious trouble in a congregation, some presbyteries will suggest a Stated Supply rather than an Interim Pastor and will not allow a Pastor Nominating Committee to be elected by the congregation until the trouble is settled.

Interim Pastor. An Interim Pastor is normally approved when the expectation is that the congregation will move through the pastoral search process in the usual fashion, resulting in a call to a pastor, and when interim services are needed on a full-time or part-time basis for a period of six to twelve months or more.

An Interim Pastor serving a Presbyterian congregation is ordinarily not permitted to accept a call to be the installed pastor of that congregation, and this condition may be written into the contract. In special cases, however, the Interim *may* be installed as Pastor if presbytery approves and if the Interim Pastor is absent from that congregation for six months (G-14.0513b).

Initiative for establishing the interim position may lie with the presbytery or the session. It may be encouraged by presbytery through its staff or through appropriate committees. The suggestion would normally come through COM, but occasionally the committee for mission planning or a similar committee might take such action. The actual invitation to the Interim Pastor, however, should come from the session (G-14.0513b).

The Interim Pastor

Some advantages in calling an Interim Pastor instead of a Temporary Supply are obvious. The session does not have to concern itself with frequent discussion about who will be the preacher next Sunday if there is an Interim. The major pastoral services that the congregation needs to sustain itself in a strong position are provided. Perhaps most important of all, the very title "interim" suggests that the congregation is *between* pastors, is or will be actively seeking another, and will soon be ready to begin a new chapter in its life under a strong new leader.

Circumstances When Interim Pastors Are Desirable

There are a number of special conditions when an Interim Pastor's services may be advisable. They would include the following:

1. When a pastor or staff member resigns, retires, or dies, is on an extended disability leave, or is in some other way incapacitated, and the congregation needs guidance and support in its time of grief.

2. To supplement the present staff when a church is declining or needs special expertise or new life.

3. When the leaders of a congregation or presbytery want to expand the vision of a particular congregation.

4. When presbytery has removed a pastor and there is conflict

within that congregation and hostility toward the presbytery or COM.

5. When there have been long-standing feuds or any kind of unusual crisis in a congregation's life and healing is needed.

6. At the time of a pulpit vacancy when there is a sudden change in the character of the neighborhood, or when an unusual mission opportunity arises.

7. When a congregation needs preparation for a new style of ministry, especially after a particularly long pastorate (when this is the case, the next minister is likely to be an Interim, whether intentionally or unintentionally).

8. When continuity of pastoral and administrative leadership and qualitative and quantitative improvements are desired during a pulpit vacancy.

9. When there is an installed pastor and there is a gap in the program of the church that needs attention but does not require additional permanent staff.

10. When there is an installed pastor and that pastor and session wish to test an experimental ministry for a specific task and for a limited time.

Additional dimensions of interim service are suggested by consideration of the size of the congregation seeking temporary pastoral leadership. Let us think first about the smaller church. Many small pastorless churches are struggling to keep alive. They are a major care in nearly every presbytery, and yet little has been done in recent years to revive them. With the matching of the rich background of some retired pastors as Interims part-time it is likely that spiritual and numerical growth and loving pastoral service could develop the potential in a given situation and prepare the congregation for an installed pastor. Another option for such a congregation is also the Stated Supply, but such pastors generally have very little special training to serve as Interim and usually do not see themselves in that role. Too often, the Stated Supply pastor sees the task as purely maintenance, and this may be what the small struggling church has had too much of already. What is more likely to meet the needs of a viable small congregation is a pastor trained in guiding planned change in a parish church, someone with experience in a wide variety of positions: in other words, an Interim Pastor.

Now consider briefly the needs of a larger church. When a sizable church is without a pastor, it is advisable to consider a variety of possibilities for interim service. One pastor could serve as the Interim with the primary assignment being the sustaining tasks, worship, preaching, and pastoral care, while another could be called as a consultant on a particular problem, whether it be conflict management or some other concern. Such a consultant might be employed for only a short time to deal with the particular problem at hand, whereas the regular Interim could stay on to offer a measure of continuity and stability to the congregation until the new pastor arrived. Churches with a multiple staff at times find it helpful to call two or three Interims. One serves as head of staff and the others as associate Interim Pastors, each with clear job descriptions and accountabilities.

In almost every kind of vacancy, whether from relocation, illness, or other particular need, an Interim Pastor can be helpful. Presbytery representatives should present clearly to the session of a church considering an Interim the benefits that an Interim Pastor can bring where there are special leadership needs.

Some presbyteries feel so strongly that Interim Pastors are desirable in every pulpit vacancy period that they have made it standard practice to require Interims wherever there is a Pastor Nominating Committee at work.

Advantages

A key advantage of the Interim Pastor's work is the objectivity and opportunity that come with its temporary character. The experienced Interim Pastor is more free than most installed pastors to deal with a congregation's grief over the loss of the previous pastor. Concerns arising out of the previous pastorate can be worked through to help the congregation avoid projecting past difficulties on the new pastor and enter the new relationship with fresh hope, vision, and confidence.

It is often easier to make significant changes in the congregation because the Interim is free from a long-term personal investment. Also, the congregation may try out, on a low-risk basis, other leadership and new styles of ministry and worship.

Churches have also experienced other advantages in using an Interim Pastor. The Pastor Nominating Committee is more likely to be free to work carefully and without undue pressure from the congregation or the session. Worship attendance level is generally maintained and sometimes increased. Congregational life keeps vital and gains direction because the Interim can provide continuing support and leadership for existing programs and services and provide *some* creative innovations if desired. A good Interim Pastor often will serve as a specialist in stewardship, Christian education, development of administrative manuals for use of sessions, and the like. In addition, the Interim, by listening carefully, can call attention to familiar and therefore tolerated abuses, such as needed building repairs, accepted interpersonal alienations, ineffective programs, and neglected areas of congregational life.

Financial giving often stabilizes and sometimes increases. The Interim gives the benefit of accumulated wisdom from previous situations and provides a fresh perspective on this church's life and mission. If the Interim makes a special effort to build trust between the congregation and the presbytery, then the presbytery can be experienced as genuinely positive, supportive and caring. It can be a time to strengthen connectional ties by involving governing body staff and some other guest preachers in interpretation of the broader church.

Above all, in most cases, the Interim's chief goals are to provide leadership during the pulpit vacancy and to prepare the congregation for the next pastor.

What an Interim Pastor Should Not Expect to Do

An Interim Pastor:

> Should not operate independently from COM or the session
> Should not support one group in a power struggle over another
> Should not ordinarily be expected to advise the Pastor Nominating Committee unless requested to do so by COM
> Should not promote any particular candidate for the pulpit
> Should not consider being, or be considered as, a candidate for installed pastor
> Should not ordinarily initiate major long-range programs or structural revisions in a congregation's organization

Not a Candidate for Vacancy

The Interim Pastor is not to be considered as a candidate for the vacancy except as provided in the *Book of Order*. The COM or the moderator should explain this to the session and the congregation. It is wise for the Interim Pastor also to make this clear to the congregation when introduced and at other appropriate times.

Experience indicates that no matter how often the session and congregation are told that it is unwise or impossible to extend a permanent call to an Interim Pastor, pressure will still be on the Interim to consider such a call. Some reasons for this were listed in an issue of the Interim Network newsletter, *The In-Between Times*. The Rev. Clark Hargus, an Interim Pastor for the Disciples of Christ, wrote:

> 1. The competent Interim Pastor is a model of effectiveness, and the people begin to see values in the Interim which they want continued. Good relationships are built and the Interim congregation does not want to face the grief of breaking ties.
> 2. There is less risk involved in keeping the Interim Pastor than in hiring someone unknown. Most churches have made mistakes in calling pastors, and they do not want to risk making another.
> 3. It would be convenient and less expensive to keep the Interim Pastor.
> 4. Interim ministry as a professional clergy choice is not understood by the laity. The professional Interim Pastor is relatively new in the church. Until the professional choice is understood, the people will think that one in interim work is looking for something permanent. Naturally they will think permanence is the preference and try to help by hiring the Interim.

This is one of the most difficult issues in many interim assignments. If the Interim Pastor does a good job or even an average job, some members of the congregation or of the session are likely to suggest that the Interim become the installed pastor. For the person committed to true interim ministry as a vocation, this suggestion can only be a snare or a distraction from the primary goal. Further, the Interim's candidacy is sure to confuse the session and the congregation as to the Interim's own goals and purposes; it will confuse the issue as to the proper goals and purposes for the congregation in this period; and it will develop hidden agendas in so many people that rational, objective, and unencumbered decision making becomes nearly impossible. In addition to diverting the Interim Pastor and the session from the real goal of the interim period, such talk begins to politicize the congregation and perhaps even the session. Such a candidacy nearly always divides the congregation.

For the Interim Pastor to become a candidate short-circuits the work of the Pastor Nominating Committee and often creates deep resentment. Experiences of this sort have led many presbyteries to require that Interim Pastors sign a firm agreement at the beginning of the work stating that this Interim will not be a candidate for this pulpit.

An Interim Pastor who openly or secretly desires to become the installed pastor has already lost the objectivity that is one of the position's major advantages. The Interim Pastor who wishes to be pastor now must be careful not to offend "important" persons or groups in the congregation. If education, discipline, mission development, conflict resolution, or other changes are needed, the Interim Pastor who wants to be a candidate is not likely to jeopardize the chances of getting a call by risking direct confrontation. Prophetic but unpopular leadership or preaching may be needed but not provided. Such considerations do not face an installed pastor in the same way. The installed pastor already has the call. The differences in the dynamics of the two situations are considerable, and few humans are truly above the kind of temptations toward blandness and "safety" that the Interim Pastor faces.

In addition to objectivity, another key word in the Interim Pastor's relationship is integrity. The interim position was created as an intentional and specialized form of ministry and should be undertaken in that spirit. Experience indicates that churches thrive best when the expressed intentions and purposes of interim ministry are faithfully honored. The Form of Government of the Presbyterian Church allows for a measure of grace when individuals or governing bodies make mistakes or when their vision changes. A six-month cooling-off period, away from the parish concerned, is a good test for any Interim Pastor who would be a candidate. In order to avoid confusion, individual presbyteries should clarify their own policies with regard to how such matters will be handled.

One Presbytery has adopted the following policy:

> Should a desire arise to consider the Interim Pastor as a candidate for the installed pastorate, permission must be obtained from COM prior to any discussion taking place. The six-month rule (G-14.0513b) must be followed in order to protect all parties concerned and provide for an open process. This means that the Interim Pastor will have to leave the congregation, with no consideration as a candidate given to the Interim Pastor until at least five months following the termination of the interim relationship. Following this process does not obligate the Pastor Nominating Committee to call as pastor the person who has recently served as their Interim Pastor, nor does it obligate the former Interim Pastor to accept such a call if it is offered.

2

Understanding
Interim Ministry

Interim Pastors, or persons who serve in very similar functions to those described in this manual, have been part of Presbyterian church leadership since our earliest years. Today we realize that a temporary pulpit supply is by no means the equal of an experienced, trained specialist in interim ministry. The development from the one to the other has been a slow process. Interim ministry as a specialty has matured as the church has grown in numbers and diversity, as church programs and pastoral care services have become more complex and varied, and as governing body executives and officers in congregations have realized the special needs almost any congregation will have when it lacks an installed pastor. Changes in the secular society around us, new learnings, and new appreciation of the dimensions of interpersonal relations and group dynamics all have helped the church to think more carefully about the "in-between time" and the opportunities and dangers it presents.

Presbytery, synod, and General Assembly leadership for the most part now realize that any organized approach to a personnel service for church leaders needs to provide for appropriate temporary leadership while a search committee is at work. General recognition of the role of the Interim Pastor and the consequent need for a better understanding of that role have followed behind the recognition by the churches of their need for a better understanding of the installed pastor's role.

One of the first organized efforts to study the role of the Interim Pastor was initiated by the Alban Institute in Washington, D.C., early in the 1970s. Monographs, guides, books, and at least one tape cassette were issued by Alban in the mid-seventies, and these are still among the best resources available. The Alban Institute was also responsible for calling together the first Interim Pastors conference, which was held in 1975 near St. Louis. Presbyterians have been represented and supportive in all the Alban Institute programs related to interim ministries and have also begun their own seminars and study programs at both Ghost Ranch and Montreat, in several synods and presbyteries, and at some seminaries.

The development of matching and placement services for interim ministries in Presbyterian churches has been a gradual process. In the 1950s the Department of Ministerial Relations (then in Columbus, Ohio) and the Commission on the Minister and His Work (in Atlanta) kept a roster of pastors, primarily retired, who were interested in interim service in parishes. These services have now been expanded and will be described later in this manual.

Some synods have given special encouragement and support to Interim Pastors or to ministers considering such service. One of the earliest efforts along this line was in the Synod of the Pacific. A cadre of Interim Pastors was organized in the mid-seventies at the initiative of Richard Moore, under the leadership of James Memmott, for guidance and nurture of the members of the cadre. Many other synods now have similar programs under way or in the planning process. One of the most complete and effective such programs is in the Synod of Lincoln Trails.

Most Protestant denominations with call systems, in which the congregation or a local parish board elects its own pastor, are now using some kind of Interim Pastor program to guide congregations through the search period. Experience has proved the benefits of the Interim Pastor plan. The prospects are good that the use of Interims will continue to grow.

A Very Short Theology of Interim Ministry

Understanding interim ministry means, first, understanding ministry and, second, understanding how ministry is modified when it is consciously undertaken at a specific place for a limited time and purpose. Every member of the church is a minister called to serve that faith which all believers in whatever time and place share in Jesus Christ our Lord. Edward Huenemann reminds us that this means a personal commitment, not to some private faith but to a universal, catholic faith. Further, this ministry is not only to a local congregation of Christians but to an apostolic church, a church *sent* and on the move throughout the world. The itineration of the early apostles in the then known world was the visible evidence of the early church's apostolic nature.

Interim Pastors today (because many of them are highly itinerant) share a special, privileged calling much like that of the apostles Peter and Paul, Silas and Barnabas. A real sense of commitment to a special mission is needed for an Interim Pastor to be willing to move every year for several years in a row.

These "marks" of the church, catholicity and apostolicity, are essential criteria for its ministry. All pastors, whether installed or interim, are called to serve the common universal faith (catholicity) and the outgoing mission-minded church (apostolicity). An Interim Pastor's ministry is specialized because it is more clearly defined as to duration and scope and because it is more focused on particular tasks to be begun and completed in a limited time.

The installation of every pastor is full of promise and danger. The promise rests in the opportunity the pastor's leadership can provide for the people's participation in the catholicity of the faith and the apostolicity of the church. The danger in every installation rests in the temptation of any congregation to assume that because they "have" a pastor, this pastor is now obligated to serve the parochial interest of the people of the congregation and not the catholic interest of the faith or the apostolic interest of the church. Quite imperceptibly, self-service can replace calling in the nature of the church's ministry.

For this very human reason, having an Interim Pastor (an apostolic visitor) in a local congregation, at the invitation of the session and the assignment of the presbytery, is significant. This transitional presence provides both continuity and symbol for ministry. The notion that installed pastors "have" ministry on a permanent basis is a dangerous illusion. An effective interim pastorate can be an excellent reminder that every congregation needs to be on the move, needs to become apostolic and risk being sent into the world to discover the universal truth (the catholicity) of the Christian faith. Without concrete change in a congregation's pastoral leadership from time to time, it could easily settle for less than the experience of the holy catholic and apostolic church.

Interim Ministry

Every ministry is limited by time and scope. What is distinctive about interim ministry is that termination is specified at the beginning. Further, there are specific tasks assigned by the presbytery or the session. This assignment is usually more limited than that of an installed pastor. In some cases the Interim is even specifically requested *not* to undertake certain pastoral tasks. All of this is designed to accomplish selected purposes, during the time of transition in preparation for another leader.

Biblical Precedents

Biblical precedents come easily to mind. *John the Baptist:* "The man who will come after me is much greater than I am" (Mark 1:7, TEV) and "Get the Lord's road ready for the Lord; make a straight path for him to travel!" (Mark 1:3, TEV). John had his own special tasks, to preach repentance and to baptize those who believed. These very acts were to prepare the people for a new day and new leadership. At the end of a relatively brief ministry, John pointed to one who was called by God to take up ministry among the people. His words about Jesus then were, "He must become more important while I become less important" (John 3:30, TEV).

Jesus' ministry was distinctly interim and itinerant. He never established a home for himself. His active ministry covered only three years. As he traveled throughout the countryside and in the villages and cities, he was constantly preparing disciples to succeed him. "Whoever believes in me will do what I do—yes, he will do even greater things, because I am going to the Father. . . . I will ask the Father, and he will give you another Helper, [the Spirit of Truth,] who will stay with you forever. . . . The Helper, the Holy Spirit, whom the Father will send in my name, will teach you everything and make you remember all that I have told you" (John 14:12, 16, 26, TEV). Jesus spoke these words to all Christian believers, and they apply to installed pastors as well as Interim Pastors.

Another perspective on a theological understanding of interim ministry today has been suggested by Frederick E. Christian, a well-known Interim Pastor, who wrote that his favorite reference suggestive of the tasks and the problems an Interim faces is the Corinthian passage in which Paul writes, "I have planted, Apollos watered; but God gave the increase" (1 Cor. 3:6, KJV). In other words, Paul saw his mission as a shared ministry, a continuation of the work performed by others earlier, to be taken up by yet other ministers later on, in all of which the grace of God was at work. In many of his letters Paul delineates the very problems an Interim faces frequently today. For example, in 1 Corinthians 1:10–13

(TEV) he wrote, "By the authority of our Lord Jesus Christ I appeal to all of you, my brothers, to agree in what you say, so that there will be no divisions among you. Be completely united, with only one thought and one purpose. For some people from Chloe's family have told me quite plainly, my brothers, that there are quarrels among you. Let me put it this way: each one of you says something different. One says, 'I follow Paul'; another, 'I follow Apollos'; another, 'I follow Peter'; and another, 'I follow Christ.' Christ has been divided into groups! Was it Paul who died on the cross for you? Were you baptized as Paul's disciples?"

Developing this theme further in 1 Corinthians 3:3, Paul writes, "You still live as the people of this world live. When there is jealousy among you and you quarrel with one another, doesn't this prove that you belong to this world, living by its standards?"

The apostle also recognizes that there are termination points in every ministry; we read frequently in the Acts how Paul worked and preached for a limited time in many cities throughout Asia and then moved on, providing for others to take leadership in ministry (Acts 13:1–3; 14:1–3; and especially Paul's farewell to the Ephesian elders, Acts 20:17–38).

Old Testament leaders often modeled similar patterns. They were not always happy to give up leadership roles, but knowing this to be God's will for them they passed on the mantle of authority.

Margaret Morris and Joan Mabon have written in the Interim Network newsletter, *The In-Between Times:*

> Perhaps more than any other, the biblical motif "wilderness" emerges most strongly as the metaphor for a congregation between installed pastors. "Wilderness" is that place of sudden freedom, uncertain leadership, changed relationships, possible deprivation—temptations, hopes, and disappointments. That place where all old fears reappear most threateningly . . . the frustrations of the present become more obstinate . . . but where all the hopeful futures take on new promise. "Wilderness" becomes a paradigm for the interim time.

Because all congregations must eventually endure the wilderness experience, they need, especially at such times, leaders who understand the wilderness, persons capable of making it a positive and productive experience.

Experienced or trained Interim Pastors know that "wilderness" is the setting for storytelling. The interim period is the time for the congregation to retell its own history, to rephrase its ancient stories, to deal with its doubts: "Weren't we better off back there?" It is time to face the fearsome obstacles that lie beyond the river, to prepare to claim Canaan at the journey's end. Morris and Mabon continue:

> The lively Exodus accounts, the Deuteronomic retelling, even Second Isaiah's gracious return from Exile—all these "wilderness" stories help an unsettled and fearful interim congregation know God's faithfulness, God's steadfast love.

Any congregation alternates between the need for caring nurture and the need for disciplining instruction; at the interim time, those needs become more pronounced, more extreme. The need for comforting manna may be painfully overwhelming; at the same time, the need for sharp, abrasive correction may be equally strong—and *all* those things have the urgency of *right now!* The issue becomes how to meet these conflicting needs and maintain creative tension between the two approaches. One Interim Pastor has described the prime leadership quality needed for the appropriate balancing of comfort and discipline as "tough love."

Sam Appel, a pastor in Camden, New Jersey, who is interested in the interim idea, has noted that some of the great women leaders of the Old Testament also present helpful images for interim ministry. He has written:

> Deborah, too, models the Interim Pastor (Judges 4, 5). She was a judge and a prophet in the time between the invasion of Canaan and the establishment of the monarchy. She provided to the people of God wise counsel, a plan of action, and support in carrying it out, and enabled laity to engage in ministry. Peace in the land was the result of her "interim pastorate."

Interim ministry is unique, special, noteworthy, a very particular calling. It is generally selective and focused on ministerial tasks that must be accomplished over a limited time. God often calls leaders to short-term special assignments. Interim Pastors today are the inheritors of a great calling in a great biblical tradition.

3

Qualifications, Preparation, and Placement

All available ordained ministers are eligible to serve as Interim Pastors. For pastors in the preretirement years of their ministry, this can become a new career. For those who are retired, interim service can be a satisfying way to use their gifts and experience in response to basic needs in the church. For some it will augment slender pensions. Younger persons with relatively little experience may occasionally be invited to serve as associate Interim Pastors, but such opportunities are unusual. Rarely will a person with no previous pastoral experience be asked to work as an Interim head of staff or as the only Interim Pastor of a congregation.

Missionaries returning from overseas service, military or hospital chaplains completing terms of service, or persons making career changes may be well qualified to serve as Interims. It is estimated that there are now over five hundred clergy serving in an interim capacity in Presbyterian churches. They are representative of the best of the pastoral clergy available, and a microcosm of the church at large.

Qualifications

This ministry requires a considerable degree of flexibility and, whether full-time or part-time, demands good health and a great deal of energy.

Personal Characteristics

A list of the desirable personal characteristics of an Interim Pastor would include:

Deep personal faith and commitment to Jesus Christ and the church
Warm personal qualities
Positive attitude toward the church
Common sense and perception
Sense of humor
Strong sense of personal worth and self-assurance (ego strength)
Self-awareness, especially of own working style
Ability to deal well with stress
Emotional stability
Stable yet flexible personal and family circumstances
Maturity and adaptability for short-term tasks
Mobility (geographical and psychological)
Ability to take risks, tackle the unknown, and confront problems
Patience and persistence when appropriate
Ability to ask for and use help

Professional Qualifications

Among the desirable professional qualifications of an Interim Pastor can be listed these:

Proven experience as a pastor or equivalent proven experience
A sense that interim service is a vocational choice, whether for a long term or a limited term (intentionally)
Tolerance for uncertainty in job security and term of service
Sensitivity to dynamics of termination, death, and grief
Interim Pastor training or certification
Training or experience in group process
Sensitivity to varied community norms
Thorough knowledge of, and sympathy with, Presbyterian polity, denominational programs, and linkages
Willingness to work with presbytery and receive its oversight
Flexibility and adaptability in liturgical practice
Ability to use varied leadership styles in differing situations
Skill in working effectively with the church's other staff, if any
Ability to motivate people
Ability to initiate work quickly and relate quickly to new people and new situations

Ability to diagnose organizations and develop strategies for working with them in contract negotiation; in problem solving, reconciliation, and healing; and in dealing with conflict openly and comfortably

Some suggest that it is desirable though not essential for Interim Pastors to have financial resources (other than income from interim service) and a home to which they can go during intervals between assignments. However, if such resources are not available, experience indicates that very careful planning can usually make up for their lack.

This is a formidable list of desirable characteristics and qualifications, but note how closely it compares with what the U.S. State Department is said to be seeking in foreign service officers: "An ability to write and talk, to analyze, to adapt and to judge, to lead, negotiate and mediate, resourcefulness, innovation, stability and adjustment, political sensitivity, interpersonal awareness and skill, planning and organizing ability, independence, perspective and breadth of knowledge, motivation, problem-solving ability, and finally, but not least important, a sense of humor." One would need a sense of humor, after reading these lists, to be considering either the foreign service or Interim Pastor service! Of course, few assignments would require that the Interim Pastor have every one of the qualities and skills mentioned.

Research by the Alban Institute suggests that there are times when the best course for a congregation is to employ an Interim Pastor for the major sustaining tasks of leadership and then to call in skilled consultants for short-term contract assignments such as conflict resolution, management of specific changes in the congregation, or the development of new programs. Most congregations, however, seem to prefer one person to handle these tasks, if possible, and will usually look for someone with the competence to do so.

How Does One Become an Interim Pastor?

Prayerful consideration of the possibility of this form of ministry should include study of the scripture and the theological foundations suggested in chapter 2 and familiarization with the characteristics, qualifications, abilities, and skills needed for the task. After some self-examination and heart-searching, a talk with someone who is engaged in interim ministry and with an executive presbyter will give a better understanding of the work and a feeling as to whether or not one is suited for it.

Training Programs

The oldest training program for Interim Pastors, and one of the most fully developed, is that conducted by the Mid-Atlantic Association for Training and Consulting in Washington, D.C. The Alban Institute, a pioneer in the field, has transferred all its Interim Pastors' training to this association and to the Interim Network. The addresses of both of these organizations are listed under "General Resources" in the bibliography.

Both the Interim Network and the Mid-Atlantic Association offer two-week two-phase programs of intensive training for Interim Pastors and vacancy consultants. The goals of their programs are to help Interim Pastors to:

1. Know some of the dynamics of termination and institutional grief processes and how to deal with them
2. Be able to assist the local church to use the vacancy situation as a period of significant parish development
3. Know the stages a church goes through while vacant and the roles of consultant and Interim Pastor in each of those stages
4. Learn how to relate to a congregation so its sense of self-determination is enhanced and a minimum of dependency on outside persons and resources is established
5. Be able to assist in starting a creative relationship between the congregation and the new pastor

Derivative training programs have also been conducted by the Synod of Lakes and Prairies, the Synod of Mid-America, and the Synod of Lincoln Trails; locally designed training events have been conducted by the Synod of the Pacific and the Synod of Southern California and Hawaii and by one or two seminaries. Additional study opportunities are occasionally presented by other presbyteries and synods. Interested pastors should inquire in their own presbytery or synod offices for guidance in finding the best places for training.

It has been suggested that there ought to be regular regional training events for Interim Pastors and that an annual training event should be held for middle governing body staff responsible for interim services and programs. Since most denominational seminaries have continuing education programs, each seminary should consider designing courses that better equip pastors to serve in interim situations. Courses already offered in the curriculum would be appropriate for this purpose in some cases. Governing body staff and other interested persons should work with the seminaries in such an effort.

The Alban Institute initiated the formation of an ecumenical network for Interim Pastors. This Interim Network publishes an occasional newsletter called *The In-Between Times,* which has as part of its aim to support and provide news about training for Interim Pastors. Subscriptions to the newsletter are available only to those who join the network. (See bibliography for further information.)

There is a move to develop standards for certification of Interim Pastors. Work is going ahead on this concern in several denominations and their agencies and in the Interim Network. Persons interested in possible interim service in churches should keep in touch with professionals in the field to learn what is happening with regard to certification. Developments in this matter may have considerable impact on the practice of the art.

Placement

Ordinarily interim assignments are arranged directly through a presbytery office. Churches are often matched with Interim Pastors who live in the same presbytery or nearby. Pastors desiring to enter interim service should first consult their own presbytery or synod. For those willing to serve beyond their own presbytery, placement services are available for interim assignments through the General Assembly's Personnel Referral Services office. Most interim calls are for six months to one year. Occasionally they are extended. Persons considering careers in interim service, or a series of interim calls, face the prospect of frequent moves perhaps over great distances in order to find "steady" employment. Some consider this an advantage and find interim service exciting because it enables them to experience different communities and cultures. One pastor put it this way: "Be an Interim and see the world!"

Another question that takes on serious meaning for Interim Pastors is housing. Manses are sometimes available, but at other times a house or apartment must be rented. The quality of housing will vary and in extreme cases may be a single room or a studio apartment. How much local help will be available to the Interim in any house or apartment hunting is another question. Experience varies, but usually parish committees or individuals will offer whatever assistance is needed. If a manse is used by the Interim Pastor, it generally must be vacated in time to prepare for the incoming pastor.

These realities mean that placement for an Interim Pastor is just as complex as it is for other pastors. The Interim Pastor will consequently want to use every resource for placement that is available.

Pastors desiring or willing to serve interim assignments should prepare a personal information form (PIF) and send the original to the General Assembly Personnel Referral Services office. They should also send copies to their own presbytery and synod offices. The best interim PIF will be as complete as one prepared for a regular call. While most session committees are willing to accept somewhat abbreviated PIFs from Interim Pastors, short forms are generally more difficult to prepare than standard ones. When only a few things are to be said, those few must indicate clearly and concisely why one desires to be considered for interim assignments.

Opportunity lists of interim positions are not published by any General Assembly office. Such positions are generally filled so quickly that the list would soon be out-of-date. This means that Interim Pastors need to be both diligent and vigilant in placement matters; otherwise they may have extended periods without opportunity for service.

Continuing Support

The Interim Pastor program is now in what might be described as an adolescent stage. Church leaders are becoming more aware of the fact that Interim Pastors can be of great value to congregations and presbyteries. These leaders also find that recruitment, training, and placement services are not adequate to current needs. Wider and better recruitment, screening, and training of Interim Pastors and more efficient and effective placement systems and services are urgently needed throughout the church. Further, governing bodies and sessions employing Interim Pastors should give more careful attention to the personal needs of Interim Pastors and their spouses both as professionals and as private persons. The life, after two or three successive interims, can become lonely and disorienting. The need for personal support under these conditions is critical.

In response to these needs, some synods and a few presbyteries have organized "cadres" of Interim Pastors who meet occasionally for mutual support and guidance. Other suggestions for developing supportive programs will be found in chapter 7.

How Does a Church Find an Interim Pastor?

Care should be exercised in the selection of Interim Pastors. It is important for all persons involved to recognize that there are individual and differing responsibilities for the Interim Pastor, the presbytery, the COM, the session, and the congregation. When the session decides in cooperation with COM representatives that an Interim Pastor is needed, it must determine what type of interim service is called for. Maintaining the regular program of the church will be essential. Consideration should also be given to the possible need for grief resolution or conflict management or healing to reconcile serious differences that may exist in the congregation's life. The possibility of development and change in a church's life at this time should be examined as well. Some combination of these tasks will help to define the Interim Pastor's responsibility.

A complete position description, with concise terms, should be developed by the session and approved by the presbytery committee. Only then is a session ready to begin the search for their Interim Pastor. Some presbyteries and synods have lists of available Interims and will be glad to consult with sessions about persons who may be a good match for a particular congregation. It is not necessary for the session to prepare a complete Church Information Form in order to get PIFs from the General Assembly office, but it is wise to give as much information as possible about the general situation, the kind of Interim Pastor desired, including specific skills, the salary that can be anticipated, and the kind of housing arrangements.

When this information is received at the General Assembly office, a search is made among those who have expressed interest in interim service and who seem to have the skills needed. The PIFs of those selected are then sent to the presbytery office or to the persons designated by the COM. Occasionally PIFs are sent directly to the session, but only if the COM approves.

One recommended procedure is for COM to provide the session with a choice, suggesting several names of persons available, including, when appropriate, those willing to undertake part-time service. In some presbyteries just one pastor's name is suggested to the session seeking an Interim. Only if that person is rejected after an interview with the session does the presbytery suggest another name. The session's first contact with a pastor should normally be through COM. How their session completes its screening and calling of the Interim Pastor will depend on what advice the presbytery offers. At times this process will parallel what a Pastor Nominating Committee does in calling an installed pastor, except that the Interim calling process must be faster and is therefore condensed. While calling an installed pastor may take nine to twelve months, the process of calling an Interim usually requires a maximum of six to eight weeks once the session and the presbytery have agreed that an Interim should be employed.

Negotiations with a particular pastor concerning the terms of an interim contract are carried out by session representatives in consultation with the presbytery. At this point it may be appropriate to adjust both the position description and the terms of the contract together, with the person the session wishes to engage. More details about contracting will be found in chapter 6.

In those presbyteries where lists of local Interim Pastors are not yet available, the COM or the executive may want to consider procedures for developing and maintaining a list of qualified persons willing to undertake interim ministries. One presbytery executive has suggested the following process for this purpose:

1. Pastors already members of the presbytery and willing to consider interim service are asked to submit a one- or two-page PIF or résumé giving their background, skills, and availability. (See Appendix C.)

2. These pastors are then interviewed by the presbytery COM. If the persons interviewed are acceptable to the COM, their names are put into the Interim Pastor cadre or roster for the presbytery.

3. Pastors who are not members of the presbytery but are willing to serve there are asked to submit a complete PIF. Such a form may be obtained from the General Assembly offices or may come directly from the pastor. When the PIF is received, reference checks should be made by someone representing presbytery or COM and a telephone interview conducted with the prospective Interim Pastor before adding the name to the list. Until the interim program is better established it would be helpful, in many cases, if presbyteries were willing to take such initiatives as these with their own continuing members.

Affirmative Action for Equal Employment Opportunity

A number of presbyteries and synods have used the Interim Pastors program to promote affirmative action for women in ministry. In at least five or six presbyteries and in two or three synods special positions have been established on a three-year plan wherein a woman minister-at-large who is a member of the presbytery or synod staff spends most of her time in service as an Interim Pastor in individual congregations. Often the pastor is called upon to serve the synod or presbytery in affirmative action work concurrently with interim ministry. This program has served to introduce some very effective women ministers to those congregations. The program has been helpful in increasing the exposure and expanding the opportunities for women pastors.

Racial-ethnic pastors are also available to be considered as Interim Pastors and are serving in a number of presbyteries. Some of their PIFs are available from the General Assembly office.

Presbyteries and synods should continue to consider affirmative action programs of the church at large as they expand their own Interim Pastor cadres and programs. Relevant *Book of Order* sections are G-11.0502e, "It [COM] shall counsel with sessions regarding stated supplies, interim supplies, and temporary supplies when a church is without a pastor," and G-11.0502f, "It [COM] shall provide for the implementation of equal opportunity employment for ministers and candidates [and] shall report to presbytery the steps in this implementation taken by the calling group." There are now pastors in almost every affirmative action category—racial ethnics, women, single or divorced pastors, and some with disabilities—pastors who are deserving of special advocacy efforts and who can make a major contribution to the life of a presbytery and its congregations by their special gifts for interim ministry. They are a resource of strength and inspiration that the church neglects to its own considerable loss. Wise church leaders, elders, pastors, and administrators alike are continuing to make diligent efforts to find and employ these specially gifted pastors in interim ministry. They need and are worthy of the churches' widespread affirmative support.

4

The Work
of an Interim Pastor

In the first conference about Interim Pastors sponsored by the Alban Institute at Thompson House near St. Louis in 1975, those present developed a description of five stages of an interim pastorate.

Stages of an Interim Pastorate

Stage 1: Pre-entry
Average time: 3 or 4 days to 3 or 4 weeks

Certain things need to occur even before the Interim Pastor has contact with the congregation. Presbytery policy about the use of the Interim Pastor needs to be clarified. The Interim Pastor needs to develop a trust relationship with the presbytery executive. The Interim Pastor, the executive, and any available consultative resource persons need to know about each other and how to use and support each other effectively; the Interim Pastor needs to learn as much as possible about the church and then to consider very thoughtfully how to get in, be there, and then get out. The governing body representatives, as well as the session, should share with the Interim any specific expectations or particular problems that need to be acknowledged or dealt with during the interim time. Guidance should be given to the Interim as to what should have immediate attention, since there will be only limited time to deal with any issue. The Interim Pastor ought to be encouraged to look upon such guidance as valid and helpful and in no sense a threat to, or an interference with, the ministry to be performed.

Stage 2: Entry

Average time: 3 or 4 weeks

Entry involves contract negotiations with the presbytery, COM, and the session of a specific congregation to be served. It demands that the Interim Pastor, the session, and the presbytery have a clear understanding about the character of this relationship. Primary contracting is usually done between the Interim Pastor and the session but always with the presbytery's advice and counsel. The presbytery executive and/or representatives from COM may meet with representatives of the session and perhaps with the Interim Pastor under consideration to develop a lucid, concise statement about the tasks to be accomplished during the interim period, what the Interim Pastor is expected to do, what the session itself will do, and what others in the congregation or presbytery may be expected to do. Important features of the congregation's life need to be identified and some clear, short-term key objectives set for the Interim Pastor's work in a written position description. A contract dealing with salary, length of term, benefits, and the like is also essential.

This takes time and may require constant repetition and redefinition. It is part of the "psychological contract" that develops between the session, the congregation, the presbytery, and the Interim Pastor. This kind of contracting, whether it is formal or informal, occurs and reoccurs continually as the Interim Pastor meets different groups and individuals in the congregation. Clearly worded, specific position descriptions and contracts help to establish trust between the Interim Pastor, the session, and the congregation and make the special goals of interim ministry much easier to achieve.

The skilled Interim Pastor will take the first few weeks of an interim assignment to get a full perspective on the situation and to develop individually a list of goals and objectives for this particular ministry. Such a list will naturally then be checked out with the session and the presbytery to be sure everything on it is both valid and realistic. This list must be limited. What is *really* possible in the time available to this ministry? All the objectives should be measurable in some way, and they then should be ranked and weighted so that the Interim Pastor has a clear idea of what comes first and what is most critical among these objectives. Some of the most significant tasks are not necessarily ones that should be accomplished first. Such a list of goals and objectives will not be complete until the Interim Pastor and the session together decide exactly *who* will do *what*. A specific person or group should be designated as being responsible for each objective and a report and follow-up plan adopted early in the entry stage.

Stage 3: The Body of the Work
Average time: 4 to 8 months

During this period the Interim Pastor focuses on providing the pastoral functions the congregation requires, maintaining and strengthening its worship and nurture. Special opportunities are available in the interim period to deal with grief and termination, with trust, with congregational identity, and with expectations for the future. All these issues can be handled as part of the ordinary pastoral functions of an Interim rather than being developed as some kind of "new thing." The Interim Pastor's sensitivity to these dimensions in the ordinary events of congregational life will help the congregation to reflect on what is happening, what has happened, and what should happen. Such reflection will guide the congregation in its continuing development.

Resolution of conflicts and clarification of needed mission development may be part of this period.

Usually it is during this stage that the search for the next installed pastor begins. If the Interim Pastor is to have any relationship to the Pastor Nominating Committee, it must be carefully defined ahead of time. Some COMs prefer that the Interim not work with the PNC. Still, the Interim Pastor and the session have some responsibility to make sure the outline of the search process is clearly communicated to the congregation. The COM representative can define how this is to be done. Sometimes the Interim Pastor can identify information or problems that should be passed on to the COM to aid them in advising the PNC or prospective candidates for the pulpit. Whatever the COM requires, the Interim Pastor will always serve as a key member of a team that includes the session, congregation, COM, presbytery, and PNC.

Stage 4: Exit
Average time: 1 or 2 months

In the period of termination, the search process concludes and a new pastor is elected. The termination phase is used to assist the congregation to do its grief work about the Interim Pastor's leaving (and the previous pastor's leaving, too, if that still needs additional work). Then the congregation is free to enter a healthy relationship with a new pastor. The Interim Pastor works to build anticipation for the coming of the new pastor, to help the congregation clarify its expectations and deal with its anxiety. The exit stage should be a time of real celebration for everyone for at least two reasons: first, because a new pastor, the right pastor, is coming, and second, because the interim tasks have all been successfully completed.

Stage 5: Post-Termination
Average time: 1 to 4 weeks

Some kind of reflection on the whole experience is wise to ascertain if the desired objectives were achieved. Reflection and evaluation by governing body executives, congregational groups, and Interim Pastors can add a useful dimension to everyone's understanding of what happened. In particular, careful evaluation by the session of the work of the Interim Pastor and a similar review of the work of the session and of the congregation by the Interim Pastor should be the minimum, requested by the presbytery in each case.

Concerns That Need Continuing Attention During an Interim

In the Pre-entry and Entry stages, the Interim Pastor can begin to develop a checklist of concerns that will require careful attention during the interim period. Some of the more common concerns are these:

Renewing and sustaining the spiritual life of the congregation
Securing from COM adequate direction for the Interim Pastor, the session, and the congregation (if such direction is not offered by the presbytery or its representative, the Interim Pastor should ask for it)
Getting to know all the church officers as soon as possible
Facing honestly any staff problems and working out with those individuals and the session or its personnel committee ways of resolving such problems
Finding out about any events, anniversaries, or observances special to the church (lay persons ought to be involved as fully

as possible in planning and implementation of the plans for all such observances or celebrations)

Assisting in the severance of any continuing ties between the congregation and the previous pastor, especially when that pastor still lives in the area

Developing a system to maintain satisfactory pastoral calling and related services

Maintaining the quality of session members and those who serve on other church boards

Keeping membership rolls accurate and up-to-date (while this is technically the session's task, the Interim Pastor can play a supportive role in making sure it is well done before the end of the interim)

Dealing with financial problems in the church (again, the Interim Pastor should offer whatever leadership is appropriate)

Developing or maintaining an inventory of the physical plant and keeping or getting it in good condition

Unifying divisions and healing bruises, if any, within and among members of the congregation, official boards, and church staff

Repairing possible damage to relations between the congregation and the presbytery or COM

Establishing contacts to continue the church's ecumenical and community relationships

Preparing an easy transfer of allegiance of all members from the Interim to the new pastor

Speedy entry is essential. Social occasions are helpful. Early meetings of all the church boards offer the Interim Pastor excellent times to get better acquainted with the officers. The sooner the Interim Pastor can call the church officers by their first names, the easier the work will be.

Flexibility is also essential, throughout the stages of every assignment. Goals and objectives agreed upon, plans made, assignments given to specific persons or groups all ought to be open to adjustment and renegotiation if circumstances change. Integrity and dependability are essential qualities for Interim Pastors, however, and agreements, contracts, and covenants ought not to be changed unless there are significant unexpected developments and all parties agree on what changes are to be made.

Five Developmental Tasks of the Congregation

The congregation has its own tasks to work on during the time the PNC is seeking a new pastor, but most congregations are either unaware of these tasks or unwilling to assume them. Unless all five of these tasks are addressed and satisfactorily completed during the interim period, the next installed pastor is sure to have some significant difficulty within two years. The successful Interim is one who understands the five tasks and knows how to guide the congregation in its work on them. Loren Mead has described these tasks in his helpful monograph *The Developmental Tasks of the Parish in Search of a Pastor,* published by the Alban Institute. Every Interim Pastor should read it.

The five tasks named by Mead are: coming to terms with history; discovering a new identity; shifts of power; rethinking denominational linkages, and commitment to new leadership and to a new future. Understanding the nature of these tasks and how best to accomplish them are critical assignments for the session and the Interim Pastor. It is important to note that the first four tasks are not necessarily sequential. They may be addressed in a different order from that listed here, and more than one of the tasks may be undertaken by a congregation or its boards and committees at any one time.

Coming to Terms with History. About the first task, coming to terms with history, Mead has written (p. 3), "The vacant congregation that would be free for the future needs to work at understanding where it has been coming from and how it got to where it is. . . . Releasing the congregation from the inappropriate and crippling power of the past is a developmental task that comes to the fore during a vacancy. Pastors themselves are often caught up in these feelings and often do not have the psychological distance that lets them 'let go' of the people." The Interim Pastor, not having been previously associated with this congregation, is uniquely equipped to guide the congregation in its work on this task. An associate pastor or a former pastor of this congregation probably cannot have the objectivity this task requires.

Discovering a New Identity. Addressing the second task, discovering a new identity, Mead states (p. 4), "It is surprising how often congregations discover that they have been dealing with a myth that puts them out of touch with what they have become and with their world. A congregation that comes through the vacancy process well emerges with a clearer sense of its own identity—who it is in relationship to its community and what it dreams of being and doing."

Shifts of Power. The third task, shifts of power, is described by Mead in these words (p. 5); "The time when pastors change is a time when some . . . potential leaders feel a call to take on more active roles. New centers of power in the congregation coalesce. . . . This is quite healthy, but it often causes uncertainty, if not discomfort, among the old lay leadership. . . . Actually, it can be a most positive moment for them, too, if they can be helped to reexamine their own commitments and ministries."

Rethinking Denominational Linkages. The fourth task, rethinking denominational linkages, may relate in some cases to the first task, dealing with the congregation's history. "A congregation's relationships with its denomination are often heavily flavored by the pastor's passions or prejudices," Mead writes (p. 5). "When one pastor leaves, the congregation is open and responsive to denominational resources in a way that has much creativity." Now the presbytery will likely have an opportunity, perhaps not available in the past, to "communicate the richness of its heritage and the usefulness of its resources from its international, national, or regional dimensions. . . . Most congregations and denominations have a new chance for collaboration." Unless both the Interim Pastor and the presbytery are aware, alert, and responsive to this dynamic, however, the session and the congregation may lose a valuable opportunity for growth.

Commitment to New Leadership and to a New Future. Finally, the congregation has finished its developmental work only when it is genuinely ready to make a commitment to new leadership and to a new future. This fifth task has both a theological and a practical personal dimension. Now the congregation needs to understand the difference between "hiring" a pastor and "calling" a pastor. In this context, "hiring" a pastor suggests finding one who seems to be a good match to the tasks described in the church information form and making a tight contract with that person to pay a "fair" wage, which sometimes is interpreted to mean paying the least dollar amount required to get this pastor to take the job. Unfortunately, some lay people—and some pastors, too—still look at contract negotiations in this light, even in the church. From the theological perspective, the act of calling a pastor means far more than contract negotiation. "Calling" suggests two other words, "commitment" and "covenant," both of which involve the work of the Holy Spirit moving in and among the pastor to be called, the Pastor Nominating Committee, the congregation, the session, and the presbytery. Covenanting and the commitments that are involved are discussed in chapter 6 on contracts. Until the congregation understands the theological dimensions of calling a pastor, this task has not been completed.

The personal dimension of this task, of course, relates to the congregation's readiness to give up a pastoral relationship to its former pastor(s), and to the Interim Pastor also, and to commit itself to a new covenant with a particular new person, the one to be nominated by the PNC. The Interim Pastor is the best person to guide (and perhaps goad?) the congregation in the completion of this work.

But what about the commitment to a "new future"? How much can an Interim Pastor appropriately do to lead or assist a session or a congregation in defining new tasks and new forms of mission? Should not the future be kept open so that the next installed pastor can shape the congregation's understanding and expression of ministry and mission? Many pastors, both those who are installed and those who are interim, will argue on both sides of this question. Because the needs, opportunities, possibilities, and practices vary greatly from one community and one presbytery to another, a definitive answer ought not to be given to this question. How much the Interim Pastor should do can best be worked out in the pre-entry and entry negotiations with the presbytery and the session. Perhaps the only clear task for the Interim Pastor in this matter is to prepare the congregation to expect changes, both during the interim time and after the new pastor is installed.

Basic Strategies

Several basic strategies are usually reflected in job descriptions for interim pastorates. Some are called sustaining ministries and are described in helpful, supportive, strong programs and services through which a congregation's basic life is nourished, the pastoral tasks are done, and the administrative life is maintained, to be turned over largely unchanged to the new pastor. Such an interim strategy is appropriate for many congregations. Even when a church is diagnosed as "sick" by its own session or by presbytery leaders, major surgery may be unnecessary if a change of "diet" and the right kind of "exercise" will do the job.

Other situations may call for specialized skill in handling complex issues that require change, clearing up deep hurts from previous conflicts, or healing long-standing feuds. (This may become a special kind of grief resolution.) Any sort of unusual crisis— such as public disgrace of the previous pastor or a congregational split—would call for a change-oriented Interim Pastor. Environmental factors, too, might make an interim pastorate a useful mission strategy, as in situations where congregations are facing decisions about whether or not they ought to be dissolved or where a sudden change in the character of the neighborhood or an unusual mission development opportunity appears at the time of a pulpit vacancy.

Interim Pastors, presbyteries, and sessions, too, need to understand what makes for a healthy relationship between maintenance and change. Every system tends to organize and hold together community life in a maintenance stance. Every organization also has tendencies to change its life. Building on a model used by the Alban Institute, a schematic way of thinking about a continuum of maintenance and change will help set these different roles in context. In the diagram below, the diagonal separating the two tendencies (maintenance and change) represents the many points from which the pastoral tasks of the congregation can be approached.

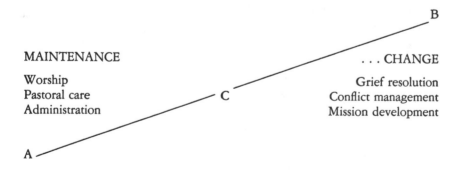

Point A is the characteristic stance of that Interim Pastor whose role is thought of entirely as maintenance, one who "holds the place" for a time. Point B, the opposite extreme, represents the role of the consultant who, having practically no commitment to mainte-

nance functions, makes interventions calculated to assist the organization or community to make changes in its life. Most Interim
Pastors would operate somewhere between these extremes, probably working closer to Point A, depending upon their skills, interests, and understanding of their role and the needs of the situation.
The installed pastor would ordinarily operate at some hypothetical
Point C, toward the center of the diagonal.

The concerns for maintenance and for change are both appropriate. The style and skill of the Interim Pastor and the needs of the
particular situation dictate the mix of maintenance and change concerns that are wise for a specific pastorate. Many believe that there
is a place for the Interim whose focus is purely on maintenance, just
as there is a place for the one whose primary responsibility is to be
a catalyst for change. Some knowledgeable Interims assert, however, that because seeking a pastor is itself a new and change-
making experience for a congregation, there is never a congregation which requires *only* maintenance services from its Interim
Pastor. If there are diverse needs in a large congregation, there is
the possibility that the various tasks can be carried out by a team
of Interim Pastors. This has worked quite well in a number of
places. It is the responsibility of the session in consultation with
COM to determine what is needed in each case and then to prepare
an appropriate position description.

Sustaining Ministries

The Interim Pastor is often expected to be the principal preaching minister, the administrator, and the head of staff, to share in
some of the pastoral calling and counseling, and to moderate meetings of the session. The Interim should be welcome in meetings of
the Board of Trustees and Board of Deacons. Where there is a
multiple staff, other pastors may sometimes take turns attending
these meetings. The Interim can also be helpful by being available
for meetings of other groups, such as young people, older adults,
and singles. The Interim is expected to take the lead in the administration of the Sacraments and Ordinances of the church but should
be willing to share that responsibility with other ordained members
of the staff, if any.

It is generally agreed that the Interim Pastor's task is to provide
continuity. Congregations are sensitive to sudden change. During
an interim some will *imagine* changes in worship forms, even
though the Interim Pastor is sincerely trying to follow well-estab-

lished routines. The simple fact that there is a different pastor doing the same thing may give the impression of change. The real problem, however, may not be so subtle. Individuals, groups, or official bodies within the church may be anxious for certain changes to come to pass. Some of these may be long overdue. The Interim Pastor is wise to consider carefully with the session any proposed changes in the church's life.

The Rev. Raymond E. Kent, one of the most experienced Presbyterian Interim Pastors, speaking at one of the Ghost Ranch seminars, made the following observations about worship and preaching in the interim setting:

> The single most effective opportunity shared with a congregation is *worship*. All parts of the service may be properly utilized to provide transitional emphasis and impetus. Worship is both a sacred event and a sacred experience. It is perhaps the one area of congregational life least amenable to change. Worship is a shared link with the past, present, and future of each person's faith. It is affirmation, confirmation, and declaration. This is a time when sense and feeling are openly responsive. Each person brings a set of expectations to worship. Once these expectations are met, members of the congregation will be open and receptive to other possibilities.
>
> *Preaching* is only one part of worship, but within Presbyterian tradition it is an integral part. No one should try interim work who isn't reasonably good at sermon preparation and delivery. Effective ministry depends upon new and fresh sermons related to these people and this situation. An interim pastorate is neither the time nor the place, if indeed there ever is any place, for a cassette service diet of other preacher's sermons. The congregation faces special needs and concerns such as grief from the loss of a beloved leader, whether by death, relocation, or retirement, and this brings deep disappointment and sometimes open hostility. The host of problems that are regularly resident in any congregation are intensified in this interim period. An interim may draw on a personal sermonic file, but every sermon whether from the "barrel" or freshly forged should be sharpened to meet specific needs.

While every sermon needs to be tailored to the individual congregation, there are a number of great Bible themes and texts that may be appropriate at some point in most interim assignments. The Rev. Robert E. Buxbaum, an experienced Interim Pastor from San Antonio, Texas, suggests the following sermon themes and related texts that a preacher might develop to deal with a congregation's need to understand what is happening in the interim experience:

The Challenge of Waiting	Psalm 27
	Romans 8:14–25
A People with a Past	Exodus 3:1–6; 20:1–2
	Luke 24:13–31a
On the Need to Control	Job 38:1–11
	Mark 4:35–41
On Rediscovering the Church	Genesis 28:10–19
	Ephesians 2:12–22
	Matthew 28:16–20
Our Presbyterian Heritage	Deuteronomy 27:1–10
	Acts 14:21–23
	1 Timothy 5:17–19
	Titus 1:5–9
	James 5:13–16
	Revelation 4:1–6a

Keeping a congregation informed during the interim interval is basic. Communication will take as many different forms as are required to maintain interest, participation, and support. Attention to regular and adequate provision of information concerning session actions, news about the programs and events of the church, and some frequent word on the work of the PNC builds trust and develops confidence in the future.

Leadership training events are natural ways to maintain and strengthen the congregation's structure. Further, there is usually a need for officer training classes because many church officers are not sure of their roles. The Interim Pastor need not always be personally responsible for conducting such training but should see that it is done and done well.

Change

We now consider three kinds of "change": grief resolution, conflict management and reconciliation, and mission development.

Grief Resolution. Generally, a congregation goes through stages of grief similar to those described by Elisabeth Kübler-Ross in her book *On Death and Dying.* These stages, not necessarily sequential, include denial, anger, bargaining, guilt, and (it is hoped) acceptance. In another approach John Bowlby summarized these stages in three steps: (1) sadness and anger; (2) disorganization and depression, and (3) reorganization. Obviously there are differences in the circumstances when a congregation *wants* a pastor to leave. Then many are happy because the pastor has at last gone. There still will be grief and some guilt, however, which need the Interim Pastor's careful attention. And when a pastor of twenty or thirty years' service leaves the congregation, the need for grief work is obvious. It is essential for the Interim Pastor to be fully conscious of this dynamic in the congregation and to discuss it with the session. Pastor and session can then plan together to work through the various stages of grief in the life of the session and of the congregation.

A group of Interim Pastors in the conference sponsored by the Alban Institute in 1975 described their understanding of the church vacancy and grief dynamic as follows:

> The Interim Pastor usually enters when the congregation is in uncontrolled dependence, a situation that may be characterized as being in a "death mode." Almost any congregation that loses its pastor tends toward this kind of behavior. The task of the Interim Pastor is to assist the congregation in moving from that uncontrolled dependence, where no activity is really purposeful or effective, toward the point at which it can do what it has to do dependably, coherently, and responsibly. (This is a movement from the "death mode" regarding what is going on in the world, triggered by the congregation's loss of its pastoral leader, toward a "resurrection set" regarding the world, with the ability to look forward to what is yet to be.)

The key dynamics with which the Interim Pastor works are trust and grief. A schematic way of pointing up the dynamic quality of the interaction may be used to describe the Interim Pastor's task with the congregation.

To illustrate:

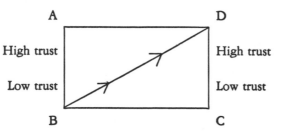

RESURRECTION SET

DEATH SET
Denial, Anger, Bargaining, Depression, Acceptance

Point B represents a kind of "death set," where uncontrolled dependence leads to a purposeless spinning of wheels. Point D represents a "resurrection set," where a congregation, increasingly able to trust itself and its world, has come to greater acceptance of loss, has worked through much of its grief, and is able to do what it has to do.

The Interim Pastor's task is to help the congregation move through the vector B to D, specifically assisting the congregation to a position of restored trust and at the same time pressing the congregation to move through its grief work. The temptation of the Interim Pastor is to build trust in the Interim Pastor on a kind of personalistic basis. This move is ill advised. It leaves the congregation doubly bereft when the Interim goes. Interim Pastors have an opportunity to use their own dependability, integrity, and professional skills to move a congregation to do its work of letting go of its past and preparing to let go of the Interim Pastor as well.

The Interim Pastor is placed at a unique point in the history of the congregation in which a kind of laboratory situation can be set up with extraordinary potential for helping the congregation discover itself and work on key dynamics of its life. The Interim Pastor can use the ordinary events of a congregation's life to actualize this laboratory experience to assist growth beyond loss, grief, and disorganization. Certain chapters in the Kübler-Ross book, as well as a number of other good books now available to help pastors understand and deal with personal grief, will richly reward the Interim Pastor with ideas that can easily be adapted to work with congregations.

Consider the following techniques:

1. *Stating* (in talks, sermons, informal meetings, and personal conversation) and *acting out* a basic acceptance that the past is gone and the future is not yet, and that it is OK for that to be the case. A sermon series helping the congregation to recall, understand, and celebrate its own history can be useful in dealing with the stages of denial, anger, and perhaps even guilt. The Old Testament is rich in stories that tell how the people of Israel dealt with some of these grief stages. Dr. Buxbaum's sermon suggestions, listed in the preceding section, effectively illustrate this point.

Family night suppers or other special programs at the church, or perhaps small-group meetings in the homes of church members, can also be opportunities to retell favorite stories about the pastor who just left and to celebrate in other ways the history of the congregation. Deliberately allowing church members to verbalize their recollections of the past can help them deal directly and positively with grief and guilt. This kind of approach would not always be wise, however, and no such program should be attempted without very careful prior consideration *with the session.*

2. *Making it clear* that the Interim Pastor is truly going to go away when the contract is over, that the departure will be real, that the Interim Pastor is not available to become the congregation's pastor.

3. *Being open,* within the boundaries of that clarity about termination, to renegotiate details of the task so that energy gets shifted to where the real congregational hurts are.

4. *Discussing and teaching* openly about death and grief.

5. *Reinterpreting* various seasons, such as Advent and Lent, to include the death/life dynamic.

6. *Dealing realistically* with the congregation's experiences of life/death/resurrection as they occur liturgically; during pastoral visits; at funerals, births, baptisms, and weddings; and when asked, "Why aren't you staying?"

Conflict Management. Churches in serious conflict or churches with major problems of other kinds are among those which have most appreciated the services of a qualified Interim Pastor. Persons who understand conflict management and are skilled in handling it can often make the difference between a relatively brief period of conflict resolution (and growth-oriented change) and a long, sometimes painful avoiding of issues and problems or a fumbling attempt to resolve critical difficulties. Generally, the course of least resistance is to pretend that conflict does not exist, or that it all centered in the pastor and will disappear as soon as the pastor is gone, or that, at the most, the differences are minor and will resolve themselves if everyone is nice. Such attitudes tend to cover up real disagreements, allowing them to fester until they erupt in major difficulty, usually some time after a new pastor is called. The wise session or COM will make sure this does not happen. Finding a skilled Interim can be the most appropriate answer to such problems in many cases. This requires careful matching of the Interim Pastor and the congregation to be served. The experienced COM will take leadership in guiding the session of such a church to persuade them that an Interim Pastor would be a good idea at this time. Finding the right person then becomes more the responsibility of COM than of the session. In such cases, both the executive presbyter and COM will find that close knowledge of their own cadre of Interim Pastors will pay real dividends. The Personnel Referral Services of the General Assembly may be helpful, too. Once the Interim is selected the presbytery's committee must trust the experienced Interim Pastor to guide the session and the congregation in identifying and acknowledging their problems and going to work on them. COM, the presbytery executive, and others in presbytery who can be helpful will naturally stand beside and behind the Interim in such a situation, making sure to provide all possible support and encouragement.

In deeply troubled congregations it may be necessary to bring in a team of Interim Pastors: a head of staff, an associate pastor, and even special consultants, all of them in interim status. When such a clean sweep was tried, everyone involved—the session, the congregation, and all the interim staff—responded wholeheartedly to what was clearly perceived as an emergency situation, and the results were gratifying.

Reconciliation. When a congregation is involved in significant difficulty, there will be need for an Interim Pastor with ability not only to manage conflict but also to promote reconciliation. Relationships with presbytery may need mending and perhaps those with other churches, organizations, or persons in the community. Objectivity and a warm personal style in working with individuals, as well as with boards and committees, are critical elements in promoting healing. It is important for the Interim Pastor to have some knowledge of the various levels and the dynamics of conflict and to know what processes promote understanding and good health in organizations. At best, the Interim Pastor will personally possess skills in mediation and reconciliation; otherwise, the Interim needs to know where to find consultants who have such skills. Everything the pastor does in the way of preaching or the conduct of worship, in the use of small groups for Bible study or other kinds of discussion, will contribute to the healing process if consciously designed to work that way.

In most cases real conflict management will require much more than reconciliation or healing. It may sometimes be necessary to bring into the open hidden conflicts or long-unresolved differences. Rarely will the Interim exacerbate or stimulate a conflict in order that problems can be identified and dealt with adequately. It would be wise for the Interim to be in frequent consultation with COM, the presbytery executive, and with members of the session about such a matter. In conflict, strong and thoughtful administrative leadership is essential.

Should the Interim Pastor become the one who will attempt mediation between parties to a conflict, a few practical suggestions as to process may be helpful. James Memmott, a presbytery executive who is also a church management consultant, told the 1981 Ghost Ranch Seminar on Interim Ministry that mediation in conflict works best when:

> The mediator is *trusted* by all parties to the conflict
>
> The mediator is *not defensive*
>
> The mediator is *deliberate* (does not move through the process too fast)
>
> The mediator is *patient* (willing to review and repeat any steps whenever that is useful)
>
> The mediator is *objective* (does not make judgments about right or wrong, does not care who wins, but rather seeks to bring all concerned parties together to help them reach agreement)
>
> The mediator is *always present* when any of the parties to the conflict talk together about it

The mediation process is generally comprised of three steps:

> 1. *Analysis:* "What's going on here?"
> 2. *Negotiation:* "What can be done about it?"
> 3. *Resolution:* "How do we settle this?"

Each step is discussed in considerable detail in what is still a standard textbook for conflict management in churches, *Church Fights. Managing Conflict in the Local Church,* by Speed Leas and Paul Kittlaus. Much of the teaching of this book is helpfully condensed in an Alban Institute monograph, *A Lay Person's Guide to Conflict Management* by Speed Leas.

At times it may be wise for the session or the COM to consider calling in specialists in conflict management or persons skilled in other kinds of organizational development to function primarily as change agents and problem solvers and to guide the Interim Pastor, the session, and the congregation in responding to special needs. A change agent or problem solver can address those things which stimulate conflict, such as:

> Inadequate communication
>
> Destructive behavior patterns

Inadequate attention to process
An organizational pattern unsuited to functions
Lack of appropriate satisfactions and rewards for members

The Interim Pastor should share fully in the planning process and welcome and work closely with any consultant who may be brought into the picture. Clear-cut written statements of responsibility and accountability for the consultant specialist and for the Interim Pastor are essential if this course is followed during the interim. A good consultant will insist on such written agreements. If that does not happen, the Interim Pastor will have to confer with governing body representatives or with the session itself to guarantee that all contracts and understandings are put in writing and honored by the parties concerned.

Mission Development. Most presbyteries insist that some kind of mission study of the church and the community be made during the interim period. This study is conducted in a variety of ways. It may be done either by a special committee, appointed by the session, or by the PNC. It may also be under the supervision and with the assistance of the strategy committee of the presbytery and COM. Such a study should include a review of the policies and organization of the congregation. It should develop long-range goals and objectives and establish ongoing processes for evaluation. It enables the session to know what its goals for ministry and mission ought to be. It enables the PNC to recognize those qualities, abilities, competencies, and experiences needed in the pastor now to be sought. The Interim Pastor should be aware of the presbytery policy and the persons and instruments used by the presbytery in this study of the church and its community. The Interim may sometimes be asked by COM to serve as a liaison or resource person in this study. When session and presbytery agree that special mission development strategies are appropriate for a congregation during the interim period, it will again be necessary to define the role of the Interim Pastor as related to changes in congregation or session goals or objectives. These are times when the Interim Pastor's task must include more than simply assuring continuity in the life of the congregation. Short-range goals and changes may be needed during an interim period. If so, they should be carefully negotiated and agreed upon by all key persons in the leadership of that congregation and presbytery. Otherwise the Interim Pastor may be setting up conditions that will lead to confusion or conflict.

If indicated by the mission study, and if initiative is taken in the right way, the interim experience may also be a time for making significant changes in a congregation's mission direction and total life. Church programs and groups already in existence may at times be used to prepare for change. In other cases, it may be wise to leave old programs and groups intact and gradually introduce new programs and new organizations for the purpose of developing change in the mission program of that congregation.

Styles and Methods

Three styles of Interim leadership may be described.

1. Consultative: Decisions are made by the Interim Pastor after consultation with appropriate groups
2. Collegial or Participatory: Decisions are made by groups or key leaders and the Interim Pastor *together*
3. Directive: The Interim Pastor takes a strong hand and directs groups in the decision-making process

The collegial or participatory style is often the one most effectively used, though the pastor's style may vary according to the particular purpose and the specific task at hand. In many troubled congregations a major part of the problem often is the leadership style of the pastor. Too many pastors are at one end of the spectrum or the other. They are too laissez-faire or too authoritarian. Rarely is either style what the congregation needs or wants, especially in an interim period. The participatory method, as a rule, best suits the Interim Pastor. One thing congregations often need during an interim is the development of more lay leaders, and the collegial or participatory style best serves that goal.

In working with some troubled congregations, however, the Interim Pastor may find that a strongly confrontive or directive personal style will get to the heart of the congregation's problems more quickly than a consultative manner. Such an approach may be abrasive; nevertheless, because the Interim is active in one congregation for only a short time, it can be tolerated for a few months and will often get the job done much more rapidly.

The Interim Pastor often discovers that many one-to-one relationships require special counseling methods and listening skills. Work with small groups not responsible for leadership or decision making also requires yet another style of leadership. The wise and experienced Interim will usually be in command of a variety of styles of working with a congregation and will adapt to the group, the individual, or the situation at hand.

5

Relationships

Interim ministries have many uncertainties. Because many Interim Pastors move frequently there is rarely an opportunity to develop long-term or close friends. Familiar faces and scenes are generally far removed. Loneliness and personal disorientation are frequent problems. Therefore it is important for all concerned to provide both a personal and a professional support network.

Support Networks for Interims

Both the presbytery and the session should have some kind of plan for the personal support of the Interim Pastor and the spouse. Such support plans need to include concern for spiritual, emotional, psychological, and other personal needs. If there are persons or groups in the congregation, the community, or the presbytery who can provide the kind of support that is needed for either the pastor or the spouse, those groups should be alerted to the need and the pastor or the spouse should be introduced to those persons or groups.

A good support network will have the following characteristics:

It is multifaceted (deals with a wide range of human needs both personal and professional)

It occurs on a variety of levels (congregational, regional, and national)

It is *always supportive* and nourishing (never punitive or draining)

It grows out of clear contracts

It recognizes that identifiable skills are necessary and applicable to interim work and provides training opportunities for pastors to develop such skills

It offers reasonable financial undergirding for professional development

Governing Body Relationships

It is important for all persons involved to recognize the individual, particular, and differing responsibilities of the presbytery, the COM, the session, the congregation, and other governing bodies in the entire Interim Pastor program and experience.

Presbytery

The Interim Pastor is one of the representatives of the pastoral arm of presbytery to the congregation. This is part of the way that presbytery cares for and supports its congregations. The Interim should always endeavor to represent presbytery as a caring, concerned community of which the congregation is a part. When a pulpit vacancy occurs because a presbytery encourages a pastor to move, or a vacancy results from presbytery discipline, it becomes imperative that the congregation experience also the broader dimensions of presbytery's interest in them. The Interim should be guided by COM and presbytery in all such matters as affect any aspect of the relationships between the session, the congregation, and the mission and ministry of the presbytery as it is shared with local churches. Many church officers and members have little more than a vague concept of what a presbytery is and does. Often they do not realize that the life and health of every congregation within presbytery bounds is of real concern. They need to know that presbytery has resources to share with every congregation: for example, staff persons, consultants, programs in leadership development, church education, stewardship, evangelism, mission, and social concern.

Membership of the Interim Pastor in the presbytery is advisable even though it is of short duration. It may be mandatory if the Interim Pastor is also to be the moderator of the session. While the *Book of Order* suggests that a Presbyterian minister who is not a member of the presbytery may be appointed as moderator of a session if there is no installed pastor there, such an appointment is at presbytery's discretion (G-10.0103). It is not wise to assume what the decision of a presbytery will be in any specific case. Close consultation with the COM is called for.

Many Interim Pastors have made it a general practice to join the presbytery where they are currently serving even though this may mean moving presbytery membership annually in some cases. Such a practice needs to be considered now in the light of the *Book of Order*'s provision for an examination of all new minister members on their "Christian faith and views in theology, the Sacraments, and the government of this church" (G-11.0402). There are a number of critical factors involved in this apparently routine matter. Both Interim Pastors and COMs will want to consider carefully the issues on both sides of the question. Should the Interim Pastor always be a regular member of presbytery? Should presbytery's examination of a proposed Interim Pastor be as thorough as for a pastor who will be installed?

Will the Interim Pastor who is not a member of presbytery receive appropriate support, guidance, and opportunity to serve on presbytery committees and possibly at synod and General Assembly? Will a nonmember support presbytery and COM when that is desired? Can COM determine whether or not an Interim Pastor is a good match for a congregation if COM has not examined that pastor carefully (as suggested in the *Book of Order* provision above)? Can presbytery facilitate the transfer of membership for an Interim Pastor speedily enough to make such transfers practical for the Interim who may have less than a one-year contract? How a presbytery decides these questions may determine both the number and the quality of those it can attract to serve as Interim Pastors within its boundaries.

Committee on Ministry (COM). A church with a vacant pulpit is assigned to the supervision of the COM; thus any interim ministry is always under its guidance (*Book of Order* G-14.0502; G-14.0513; G-11.0502 d and e). COM will find it advisable to:

Have a set of policies concerning Interim Pastors
Share in depth with the Interim Pastor its knowledge of the particular church
Interpret the role of the Interim Pastor to the session and the congregation
Describe the Interim Pastor's role in the mission study
Assist in developing the Interim Pastor's contract with the

session and interpret its terms of service and compensation clearly to all participants

Explain to all parties the ministerial ethics involved, especially the relationships of the previous pastor to the congregation

Request or require quarterly written or verbal reports from each Interim Pastor in presbytery

The Interim Pastor will find it advisable to:

Keep COM informed through regular reports

Share any significant problems in the church with the appropriate presbytery committees

Other Presbytery Committees and Councils. Some presbyteries integrate parts of the work of the COM with other presbytery committees responsible for development or mission strategy, and give them authority together to represent the presbytery in work with churches seeking a new pastor. One such model is a combination of the Congregational Development Committee and COM which supports churches by providing a vacancy team for Interim leadership (see Appendix E). This model outlines useful procedures for COM.

Interim Pastors may find valuable resources for church programs in other presbytery committees, such as leadership development, church education, stewardship training, or evangelism. All such presbytery services ought to be utilized as much as possible by the Interim Pastor and the session, for they greatly stimulate the life of a congregation.

Presbytery Staff. The Interim Pastor or corps of Interim Pastors in any given presbytery or synod needs to develop a trust relationship with the executive and other staff, as appropriate. The Interim Pastor, the executive, and any available consultative resource person need to know how to assist one another. As a rule, the initiative for such supporting relationships should be in the hands of the governing body staff persons. If necessary, however, the Interim Pastor could initiate such contact.

Session

The moderator of the session of a church with a vacant pulpit is appointed by the presbytery upon recommendation of COM. The Interim Pastor may or may not be designated as moderator, but if not moderator, the Interim would ordinarily participate in session meetings. When the Interim Pastor is a member of another presbytery than that of the congregation currently served, a working arrangement can be made with the moderator of the session and approval of COM.

Congregation

Interpretation of the Interim Pastor design and purpose should be presented to the congregation by representatives of COM and the session. They should explain how the Interim Pastor is selected. This would include looking at the position description and the contract and covenant agreed upon between the Interim Pastor, the session, and the presbytery; what the Interim Pastor does and does not do; and how long the Interim Pastor may stay. A statement should be made that the Interim Pastor is not a candidate for the permanent position. Later, a similar statement should also be made by the Interim Pastor. This will make it easier for the Interim Pastor to prepare the congregation, as well as the church staff, for the coming of the new installed pastor.

Other Relationships

Pastor Nominating Committee (PNC)

At times the Interim Pastor will be asked to become involved in the pastor-seeking process. After all, the Interim is on the job at the church, readily available for consultation, and may be experienced and knowledgeable about the presbytery's policies and practices with regard to PNCs. Further, asking the Interim to be COM's representative to train and guide the PNC may well save considerable money, time, and energy, both for the presbytery and the congregation. Occasions where this may be desirable might include these:

Congregations located at considerable distance from other Presbyterian contacts, usually in large, sparsely settled regions

Presbyteries where COM leaders are particularly overburdened at the time and no other representatives are readily available

Circumstances where the economic conditions in the congregation or the presbytery might make this a wise choice

Presbyteries where the Interim Pastor is well informed about PNC policies

What relationship, if any, the Interim Pastor has with the PNC is a decision of COM, and this needs to be made clear at the beginning of the relationship. The Interim Pastor, the session, the PNC, and the congregation all need to be fully informed as to what is to be expected from the Interim. Clarity about this is vital. Flexibility is important in this as in all matters for an Interim, however, and if any changes are desired during the course of the interim time, then, again, clarity and openness about the Interim Pastor's role are well advised. In everything the Interim Pastor should be seen as part of a team that includes presbytery, COM, session, congregation, and, in specific ways, the PNC itself.

If the Interim Pastor is to represent COM in its work with the PNC, that relationship may range all the way from close, full, and effective guidance of the PNC in all its work to a more distant, partial, and informal kind of support and limited guidance. COM should set the tone and describe the particulars of this relationship.

One pattern that has worked well assigns two roles to the Interim: resource person and coordinator. Under the first assignment the Interim provides some liaison between the COM and PNC, communicating information both ways, offering training, support, and guidance on process matters when requested, trouble-shooting if that is needed. The second role in this model, coordinating, means monitoring the relationships the PNC has with the session, the congregation, and COM. This would mean facilitating the session's work on the church information form, approval of that form, and, toward the end of the task, making sure the responsibilities of both session and PNC are honored in the completion and prosecution of the call process. With the congregation and COM, coordination might mean being sure everyone is adequately and appropriately informed as to the PNC's work along the way, especially at the time of the call itself. Any model that is adopted should be carefully described, in writing, so that all members of the team know what is expected.

In some presbyteries COM may discourage or prohibit the Interim Pastor from any work with the PNC, for various reasons. For example, the Form of Government is designed to prevent any small group of persons from taking control of a congregation for long periods of time. Rotation of lay leaders on all boards is a well-established practice. This is why our government provides that the

PNC is to be elected by the congregation, not by the session, and that its membership will give fair representation to all groups in the congregation. This PNC, elected by the congregation, reports to the congregation, not to the session. Some fear exists that if the moderator of the session is also the liaison to work with the PNC, there will be undue influence flowing from the session to the PNC through the moderator.

Some presbyteries do not want the Interim to serve as adviser to the PNC, believing that such work may interfere with the primary tasks for which the Interim has been called. Of the special tasks on which the interim ministry ought to focus, few of them relate to *choosing* the next pastor, but rather to *preparing the way.* It may be confusing for the Interim to try to assume both tasks.

Often the Interim comes from another presbytery and does not know the practices current in the new presbytery. In such cases, conflicting advice is sometimes given to the PNC. Naturally, presbyteries want to avoid the possibility of such confusion. Occasionally the Interim, with every good intention and quite unconsciously, delays the PNC in its work by continuing to suggest names of candidates for the pulpit long after that phase of the process should be completed. While it is rare that an Interim Pastor actually does confuse or impede the work of the PNC, it has sometimes happened. That is why some presbyteries advise that the Interim Pastor not serve the PNC. *Remember:* Specific advice from presbytery will always supersede any suggestions in this manual.

Church Staff

Personnel Committee important

In a church with multiple staff, the Interim Pastor's relationship to the professional staff and to the nonprofessional staff of the congregation is a major key to a successful pastorate. There must be a clear understanding with COM and the session as well as with each of the church staff members as to the Interim's responsibility and authority in staff matters. In smaller churches the same principle ought to apply. The Interim Pastor's responsibility and authority regarding either paid or volunteer staff should be explicit and be put in writing for all concerned.

As for professional staff, it is important for the Interim Pastor to understand the career and personal problems created when the head of staff leaves a congregation. The remaining staff members may feel threatened. In some cases, their jobs are at stake and their family's future unsettled, to say the least. Members of the staff may have ambitions to succeed the pastor who has just left even though the *Book of Order* prohibits that. The Interim can perform a valuable role as pastor to staff associates in such matters. The Interim Pastor should interpret the fact that the Interim's role with the PNC is one of neutrality. The Interim Pastor can be a friend and counselor to the staff in their hopes and aspirations. If a staff member needs or wants to move, the Interim can be personally supportive and should share this information with the COM when appropriate. A wise and supportive Interim Pastor will generally in turn find wise counsel and real support from the congregation's other staff members. Such relationships become enriching for all.

Previous Pastor

The previous pastor should observe all the appropriate ministerial ethics in relationship to the Interim Pastor that would apply to an installed pastor. This should be interpreted by the COM to the former pastor, the session, the congregation, and the Interim Pastor. Yet sometimes awkward situations develop. The pastor may be still in the area or may be making frequent visits in the former parish. Weddings, funerals, and other such occasions are difficult times for all concerned. In most cases, it is appropriate for the Interim Pastor to be generous in inviting the former pastor to participate. However, if there are violations of the presbytery's ministerial ethics they should be referred promptly to the appropriate committee of presbytery, in most cases COM.

Further Relationships

Synod

Several synods now provide programs for training and support of Interim Pastors, and such programs should be recognized, encouraged, supported, and utilized by presbyteries, congregations, sessions, and Interim Pastors. It is the business of COM to tell sessions and Interim Pastors where such programs exist and how to make use of them. Where synods have established interim cadres or placement services for the personal and professional support of Interims, it is especially important to be sure that such information is widely shared and the benefits made known and available to all Interims in the synod. If there are synod staff persons and committees concerned for interim programs in the local church, they should be informed of all changes in interim assignments.

General Assembly

The Interim Pastor should register with the Assembly's Personnel Referral Services. COM will want to keep the national offices informed as to who is serving each congregation every time there is a change. The offices do not need to know about Temporary Supplies but should be informed with regard to Interim Supplies and Stated Supplies.

If Interim Pastors wish to use the placement services now available through the General Assembly, then they also should notify the Assembly office each time a new interim assignment is accepted. If subsequent placement is likely to be desired, notice of the Interim's next availability date should be sent to the General Assembly office (and to selected synod and presbytery offices) at least six weeks before the conclusion of an interim assignment. This is suggested because most sessions, with presbytery assistance, are able to find an Interim Pastor in about forty-five days, or a little more than six weeks.

The Interim Pastor should take responsibility for notifying the Board of Pensions concerning place and term of service as well as compensation. The Interim should be sure that all pension dues are promptly and fully paid. Of course, this is properly the task of the congregation's treasurer, but since this person may never before have served as a church treasurer during an interim period and may be confused or misinformed about some of the details, it is wise for the Interim Pastor to take a close interest in the matter. It is also wise to ask for written confirmation from the Board of Pensions concerning all details whenever there is a change in place or terms of service. Pastors who were previously served by the Board of Benefits and Annuities in Atlanta should note that, though the name of this board has been changed, they will continue to be served from the same location as they always have been. Others will be served from the Philadelphia office.

In some congregations (generally only in the largest), pastors are given the privilege of attending the General Assembly each year as a visitor at the expense of the session or the congregation. When an Interim Pastor is contracting with such a congregation, there may be times when it would be appropriate to ask if this perquisite could be granted to the Interim. Even a few days at a General Assembly would benefit the congregation, as well as the Interim Pastor, in a variety of ways. Such a visit is nearly always stimulating to a pastor, refreshing the mind as well as the spirit. It would also give the Interim a chance to relate more closely to an informal national network of persons interested in interim ministries. Sometimes placement opportunities develop at General Assembly.

Some Interim Pastors who undertake this work as a specialized ministry have expressed regret that this vocational choice seems to have ruled out the possibility of ever being elected by a presbytery as a commissioner to a General Assembly. Presbytery nominating committees ought to take a look at this matter. It would be appropriate, occasionally, to send an Interim Pastor as a commissioner to the Assembly. This suggestion also applies to election to service on General Assembly or synod boards, committees, or ministry units.

The General Assembly offices and staff are strongly supportive of the Interim Pastor Movement, the Association of Presbyterian Interim Ministry Specialists (APIMS), and the Interim Network. This manual is one evidence of that fact. Experience suggests it can be expected that General Assembly ministry units will continue active advocacy for a variety of interim ministries in the Presbyterian Church.

Ecumenical Relationships

Of some consequence for the ongoing life of the congregation will be the posture of the Interim Pastor in relating to the clergy of other congregations in the community. As a Presbyterian pastor, the Interim will in all likelihood have an ecumenical interest and, in exercising this, may want to learn from other staff members, from the session, and from COM what direction the congregation has taken in the past and what ecumenical relationships are important, advisable, or acceptable for the near future. The Interim Pastor will want to reinforce any customary participation in ecumenical work or worship. Certainly the Interim will want, in any way appropriate . within the limits of the interval, to engage in every effort to bring to fruition the prayer of our Lord for his disciples, "That they may all be one" (John 17:21).

6

Pastoral Covenants and Contracts: Entry, Exit, Evaluation

When Abraham's God bound him to a covenant (Genesis 17), there was established a deep personal relationship growing out of a total commitment of the one to the other, with each assuming his share of responsibility for the relationship and each enjoying certain stated benefits. Abraham gave himself and his descendants completely in service to God, while God promised Abraham many generations of children and a fruitful land in which to live. This was not a temporary, interim relationship but a lifetime commitment: indeed, a commitment for all generations. Every Christian believer is today an inheritor of that Abrahamic covenant, fulfilled for us in Jesus Christ our Lord.

The Pastoral Covenant

The covenant we have, both the old covenant through Abraham and the new covenant through Jesus Christ, has set the pattern not only for our relationship with God in Christ but for all our human relationships as well. The covenant is a reciprocal, dual commitment, with a willingly assumed responsibility and a joyfully received blessing moving back and forth between and among all parties to it.

A contract between Christians becomes a covenant when all perceive that God is a party to the agreement and when there is mutual blessing and serving in action and reaction among those who commit themselves to the covenant and to each other through that covenant. Such should be the nature of a contract with an Interim Pastor, a session, and presbytery. While temporal details of the agreement are being negotiated and each party is seeking the genuine welfare of the others, the spiritual dimensions and implications of the contract must also be in the forefront of all conversations about that contract, the position description, the terms of employment, and the benefits.

When each party is genuinely seeking what will best serve the needs and reward the hopes of the others, then a covenant has been established, not just a contract.

A further distinction about a covenant is that it focuses as much on persons as on tasks to be done, and that is why a covenant can never be written in the abstract but only when a session has a particular person in mind and can shape the covenant with and for that person. A contract begins to become a covenant only when all parties thereto have a significant share in setting the terms and commitments that are to be made. While a job description or a contract can be written with no particular person in mind, such documents become covenants only after they are modified in the light of God's call to a particular individual to undertake a particular mission or ministry. A position description can be written for any job that needs doing—one can even describe ways the job could be done—but a covenant can be written only with a particular person in mind to describe what *that* person will do and the individual ways in which it will be done, *in company with* the others who are members of the covenanting community. Such ought to be the nature of all Interim Pastor agreements—not just job contracts but genuine covenants where God's purposes for a carefully selected individual pastor and a particular pastor-seeking congregation are fulfilled in interaction with and reaction to the initiative of the Holy Spirit.

The Interim's Contract

Once a particular session has decided to seek an Interim Pastor they will want to work closely with COM, not only to find the right person for the interim position but to ensure a fair and equitable contract. Probably they will want to write both a contract and, after choosing an Interim, a covenant with that person. The suggestions in this chapter are designed to cover as many different circumstances as possible. It is unlikely that any one contract will include every item listed here, but it will be wise for the session and the Interim Pastor to review carefully all the following suggestions. Before looking at the details of contracting, however, let us consider an interpretive statement from an experienced Presbyterian Interim Pastor. Raymond Kent told one of the Ghost Ranch seminars:

Interim work is, I believe, one of the most uncertain and stressful forms of ministry. The frequent moves, lack of job security, being without the more normative support systems, subjected to a constant change of doctors, dentists, community services, and the normal aggravations related to moving are a dependable source of frustration. Those who seldom move may philosophize, even sympathize, with this facet of interim ministry. You must have been there to empathize. The wear and tear on people and things, the cost beyond "moving expenses," and the effort required to make a home out of so many houses and apartments in succession are all added to the job-related circumstances.

The reason for calling attention to these matters is threefold: One, salary for any work is based primarily upon the job itself; two, both the job and job-related factors have considerable effect upon those doing the work; three, compensation is more equitable when it takes all factors into account. Remuneration should be commensurate with the total job picture. My contracts with a session include full coverage of salary and benefits for 90 days beyond the arrival of the new pastor. . . . To date, only one month of such time has been required. . . . Even though these factors are always present, they do not dominate our thoughts. We recognize the reality, we take the risk, and we live with it.

One reason Ray Kent is able to "live with it" is because he has a very able and resourceful wife, Betty, who has done much to make Ray's interim ministry possible. Whatever the pastor's resources and personal support may include, certain businesslike negotiations must be part of the contracting phase for every interim ministry. Let us look at key elements that are part of pre-entry and entry negotiations.

Negotiations

The first contact of an Interim Pastor with any church should be through the Committee on Ministry. COM should counsel with the session and the congregation before consulting with any Interim Pastor about a particular church.

The Interim Pastor may negotiate with the personnel committee of the session or with the full session. (Some details for such a contract are outlined in the next section; this contract is not final until presbytery has approved it.) The Interim should have a meeting with the entire session before the arrangements are completed in order to be sure that job expectations and other terms of the agreement are held in common.

The Interim Pastor should be certain COM has arranged for presbytery's approval in whatever way it is needed: for permission for the Interim to join presbytery, to labor within its bounds, to moderate the session, and so on. The Interim Pastor will also need to get approval to labor outside the bounds of that pastor's own presbytery or to join the new presbytery.

Finances

The level of service usually determines salary and is a matter of agreement between the session, the Interim, and COM. If only Sunday preaching is desired, a good point to begin with is the amount that the church has been customarily paying per Sunday for a preaching supply, plus travel expenses, lodging, meals, and payments for annuity or pension.

If a "full-time" Interim Pastor is desired and the Interim moves away from home, any one of four approaches might be used in beginning negotiations on salary.

1. The Interim Pastor should be paid what the predecessor was paid. If by presbytery standards this is far below what will be required to call the next pastor, then some mid-range should be negotiated. A complication here, especially for smaller churches with limited budgets, is that the costs of moving expenses both ways for the Interim Pastor and one way for the new pastor need to be provided for somewhere in the budget.

2. Another approach is to provide an amount which, with the retired Interim's pension income, would approximately equal what the Interim Pastor received during active full-time ministry.

3. The Alban Institute suggests that for retired pastors the church should offer enough so that salary payments plus the pastor's pension equal at least three fourths of what the church was paying the previous full-time pastor. This would be of particular benefit to smaller churches that need interim service. The suggestion is hinged upon the realization that the Interim Pastor cannot completely take the place of a resident full-time pastor. This total amount should not fall below the presbytery minimum, including the pension payment, if full-time service is expected.

4. Still another approach is that remuneration should be based upon the job itself, taking into account the time required, the skills and abilities needed, and the presbytery minimum, factoring the job according to your presbytery's suggestions or ones available from the Church Vocations Ministry Unit. In some presbyteries, a salary supplement fund or other funds may be available to help small churches meet the presbytery minimum.

For positions less than full time, salaries should be pro-rated: if the Interim Pastor works half time, the salary should be one half the previous salary; two-thirds salary for two-thirds time, etc.

The retired Interim Pastor's pension payments continue for a period not to exceed fifty-two Sundays in one church. This fact must always be taken into account in considering remuneration. In one sense, this makes the pension plan the underwriter of interim services. A retiree receives this pension payment whether or not that retiree is working. If the retiree serves an agency outside the jurisdiction of the denomination, the pension continues without termination regardless of the length of that service. If a person serves any Presbyterian agency or church, the pension payment to the retiree continues for fifty-two Sundays and then is terminated, unless the retiree moves to a new position in another parish. If the congregation and the Interim Pastor desire to remain in this relationship beyond the time allowed by the pension board, it is customary for some other financial arrangement to be worked out, because pension payment to the Interim Pastor will cease at that time.

It is understood that travel costs and motel expenses are the responsibility of the church when interviewing a possible Interim Pastor and that a regular honorarium should also be paid if the Interim Pastor preaches before being appointed to the position.

Contracting

A contract should be prepared either by COM, the session, or the session personnel committee, early in the process. It ought to include:

A very clear job description, spelling out what primary tasks are expected of the Interim Pastor and what is *not* expected

The lines of accountability and supervision in all directions

How and when the work is to be evaluated (details should be openly negotiated with COM and the session and then communicated to the congregation; see suggested contract in Appendix A)

Elements. Here are some of the elements that ought to be considered in these negotiations:

The Interim Pastor's relationship to presbytery: member or laboring within the bounds

Ministerial ethics of the Interim Pastor and the previous pastor

Length of time contract will run

Not available for call to that parish

Relationship to that session: moderator or what?

Staff relationships clearly defined

Relationship to PNC (through COM only?)

Relationship, if any, to a mission study, the goals and objectives of the session, or the preparation of any part of the Church Information Form

Provisions for termination by any party (Interim Pastor, session, or COM)

The session's and COM's goals and purposes in establishing this interim position

A position description, carefully detailed, possibly with some suggestions as to session's expectations concerning the time to be devoted to various job responsibilities (see chapter 4)

Terms. The terms of the contract should include all or most of the following items:

Amount of time (full-time, half-time, or other)

Salary and benefits, housing, travel, hospitalization, moving costs (both ways), vacation (one week per quarter?), continuing education (including time and expenses), pension, Social Security payments (all or part?)

Released time for special commitments to presbytery, synod, General Assembly, or other

Other conditions of service

Salary benefits when unemployed, usually only for those not retired (some churches agree to pay up to three months' salary and benefits after an interim call terminates or until the interim locates a new position, whichever is sooner; if an Interim is employed by a governing body, it would assume such costs)

Length of service (determined by the presbytery but always ending with the effective date of the call of the new pastor, if not sooner)

Interim Pastors who are retired should carefully consider Social Security benefits. All pastors are strongly urged to participate in the Social Security program. There is an allowable amount a retired person can earn annually without penalty. (It has been about $8,000 but may change.) A wise Interim Pastor will check on this matter regularly. Some contracts are developed so as to include additional compensation such as housing allowance. If the cash compensation, plus housing or housing allowance, exceeds the allowable amount, it is generally wise to hold one's Social Security checks in a separate bank account and report earnings at the end of the year. The Social Security Administration will then notify the recipient of the payment required or withhold future payments until the overage has been satisfied. (After age 72 there is no penalty placed by Social Security on the amount of earnings, but of course this policy could change in the future.)

Additional questions that need to be answered will include the following:

Are expenses paid by the congregation considered salary?

What about tax-sheltered annuities as a possible way for the Interim Pastor to receive income without exceeding the allowable amount under Social Security?

Will housing be counted as income by Social Security?

Can a church give a medical allowance within Social Security regulations?

How are wedding and funeral fees to be counted?

Can the Interim Pastor get Social Security reinstated the month after employment is terminated?

The answers to most of these questions can be obtained at your nearest Social Security office or from your Board of Pensions regional representative.

Retired persons should also study carefully all the relevant provisions of the pension plan, remembering especially that after twelve months' service the retired Interim Pastor must return to active status or conclude service to that particular congregation if pension checks are to continue.

At such a point, if the employing church wants the Interim to continue it may sometimes assume the cost of the pension and pay it to the Interim Pastor in addition to the previously established compensation in order to keep the Interim's income at the same level. This obviously exerts a certain indirect financial pressure on the PNC of that congregation to close the interim period at the end of the first twelve months, or more money must be budgeted for the Interim Pastor.

For Interim Pastors not yet retired, the congregation pays the usual pension dues calculated on the total of the cash salary, housing allowance, and deferred compensation, if any. During the time the Interim Pastor is unemployed, there are two options: continue to pay dues at the same rate as was the case in the most recent employed position, or request from the Board permission to pay dues on an "unemployed status"; that is, on an assumed annual minimum salary.

Church treasurers need to be informed about the following procedures, usually by COM or its representative:

1. If the pulpit has been vacant for a time, the church treasurer should pay "vacancy dues" of 12 percent of the former pastor's salary and housing. This continues until the date the Interim Pastor begins.

2. The church treasurer should then complete the change-order coupon with the new terms and the effective date and return it to the proper office.

3. When the Interim Pastor's relationship terminates, the church treasurer should again use the change-order coupon to notify the Board of the change.

The Entry Process

The session and COM together should have a clear understanding of who will be responsible for each part of the pre-entry and entry processes. Questions that need to be answered in specific terms include the following: Who will interpret the concept of the interim pastorate to the congregation? Who will explain what the Interim Pastor does and does *not* do, how the Interim Pastor is selected, how long the Interim will stay? The congregation should be informed as to the nature of the covenant and the contract (including the job description) that have been agreed upon between the Interim Pastor and the session.

Orientation of the Interim Pastor to the congregation and its history, to the community and its essential elements, and to the presbytery and its work should be an early part of the entry experience. A particular individual or group (the presbytery executive, COM, or some other committee or individual) should be assigned to make sure the orientation is adequate, prompt, and completed quickly.

Publicity about the coming of the Interim Pastor, including some background, should be shared with the community as well as the congregation. This will let people know that things are well in hand and moving forward.

Covenanting Service or Service of Recognition

Presbytery will want to recognize the significance of this new interim relationship by conducting a special worship service that will emphasize the covenantal nature of this unique call and involve the entire congregation in the covenant, particularly if this is the congregation's first experience with an Interim Pastor. Such a service can be designed both to inform and to inspire the congregation, the session, and the Interim Pastor. There may also be some brief, meaningful recognition of, and prayer for, the new Interim at a meeting of the presbytery as well.

Entry Checklist

This list is only a suggestion. Important items may be omitted, and some suggestions may be unnecessary in certain places. It may be appropriate to accomplish them in a different order. Some might be called "pre-entry" and should be completed before the Interim Pastor appears at the church to be served. How the list is used will vary from case to case, but it should be reviewed early in any interim negotiations.

1. What do the COM and the session expect of the Interim Pastor, and what does the Interim expect? Are the job description and the terms of the contract clearly understood by all persons and groups involved?

2. What presbytery policies apply to this relationship? What is the minimum salary? What are the other terms of the call?

3. Who is to moderate the session? Who is the COM chairperson? To whom does the Interim Pastor relate?

4. How does presbytery understand this congregation? What are its problems? What are its needs? What are its opportunities?

5. What is the congregation's structure? What are the organizations, responsibilities, and expectations of the session, deacons, and trustees respectively? What are the other significant leadership groups in this congregation? What do they expect of this Interim?'

6. What is the accepted style of administration in this congregation? Should that be changed? If a change is indicated, should it be undertaken during the interim?

7. The Interim Pastor should interview any paid staff and other persons with specific and significant roles in the congregation, such as the music director, the secretary, the custodian.

Also, the Interim should meet officers, moderators, chairpersons, and other church group leaders to determine needs and opportunities. How do these persons see their roles?

8. What policies are there regarding the use of the building and equipment?

9. What major program events are coming up? Do they follow the Christian calendar? Is there a local church calendar? What are the congregation's customs, holidays, annual events?

10. What ecumenical relationships does the congregation maintain?

11. What community relationships does the congregation maintain?

12. Secure and study the following records: financial report and budget, church directory, current membership lists, church support lists, list of organizations and their officers, personnel policies (sick leave, vacation, supplies, etc.), church calendar, mission studies or surveys, Church Information Form (when completed), and session minutes and session committee organization.

13. Determine if there is a system for notifying the Interim of pastoral care needs. If there is no such system, establish one.

14. Determine what individuals and families will need pastoral attention during the first two or three weeks.

15. What are the congregation's practices and policies regarding weddings and funerals?

16. Get acquainted with the community.

The Exit Process

The effective Interim Pastor's termination process begins at the time of the first conversation with the session and goes into full swing on the arrival to begin work at the church. It must be clear from the beginning that this is an *interim* assignment and this pastor is present to prepare the way for another. Building a strategy for termination should be part of the original conversation with the COM and with the session. In every case, the planning should relate to one of the chief goals of the Interim Pastor and of the entire interim experience—to prepare the way for the new pastor and for a new chapter in the life of the congregation.

The termination strategy can take form in a variety of ways and places. The worship service, Bible study, and other programs, even pastoral calling, can all be opportunities for preparing the way for the one who is to come. The first sermon the Interim Pastor preaches, for example, ought to say both "Hello" and "Good-bye"!

Some Interim Pastors make it their task to be sure a complete record of essential elements of the congregation's life is brought together in one place for easy use of the new pastor. A committee of the session or the deacons might do this. Such a record might include the mission of study just concluded, if it is separate from the church information form; the latest annual report of the session, the congregation, and every board committee, along with an accurate membership roll; a description of the session's present committee structure and method of operation; a statement of the church's bylaws and current policies; and church newsletters and other publications that would be of interest to the incoming pastor.

Explicit efforts to prepare the church staff for the new pastor are desirable, and discussion with the session can explore the ways in which this can be done.

The wise Interim Pastor can increase anticipation over the coming of the new pastor and also help to resolve any related possible problems. Sermons, teaching, even casual conversations can help alleviate congregational impatience and heighten healthy expectations for the coming of the new pastor. The Interim Pastor can warn against expecting too much too soon. One wise, experienced Interim Pastor reported that he once said to one of his congregations toward the end of the interim assignment, "Remember this, you cannot expect your new pastor to work the way I have here. Your next pastor will be installed and therefore will have a different situation with different relationships. She will need to work in a different way." Another said, "I have had forty years' experience in ministry. Your new pastor has had only four years since seminary. Do not expect him to act, work, or perform in the way I have."

Most Interim Pastors are more secure and comfortable than many installed pastors and they therefore appear more confident and make a better impression on the congregation and community. Depending on the length and type of a particular interim pastorate, the minister does not usually get beyond the honeymoon stage in the relationship. This means that both the pastor and the congregation have unreal assessments of each other. Like lovers who typically put their best foot forward, they experience the "other foot" only if the relationship lasts long enough. Both congregations and pastors need to understand this dynamic of the interim relationship.

Probably the best time to share this learning is as part of the preparation for the next pastor. Whoever it is, this person will not be the new Messiah that some look for. The understanding of the congregation as to the true work of an installed pastor will need to be informed and sharpened.

Sometimes an informal lunch date with the pastor-elect and a member of COM is helpful in providing insights into the church and its life. Such a meeting ought not to take place, however, unless COM approves of it first.

Exit Checklist

All relationships between the Interim Pastor and the congregation are severed upon termination of service. Some important items in an exit or termination checklist would be the following:

1. Set the termination date for the Interim in conjunction with the date of the arrival of the new pastor, probably when the arrival of the new pastor is imminent.

2. See that the records are up-to-date: financial, membership, minutes of the session and other groups, weddings, baptisms, and funerals, mailing lists, and so on.

3. Gather information helpful to the new pastor or COM. In addition to the items mentioned earlier in this chapter, this would include unusual traditions or customs in worship or social events, musical potential in the congregation, lists of people who can assist in worship services, lists of meetings of presbytery, councils of churches, and key community groups.

4. Conduct exit interviews with all church staff.

5. Make a "state of the church" report to session or congregation or COM and discuss with the COM any problems that may affect the future of the congregation. In such an evaluation, avoid dealing with personalities, except in the most unusual cases.

6. Preach a sermon on how to treat a new pastor.

7. Finally, the Interim Pastor should find another field of service and get out of this one or take a vacation—far away!

The Concluding Worship Service

The celebration of Holy Communion is especially meaningful at the conclusion of an interim pastorate, but if that is not deemed appropriate, then the Interim's final worship service should include some kind of termination ceremony. Prayers for the congregation, its leaders, and its new pastor and a farewell sermon are called for. The message might be something of a John the Baptist–type ("Your new pastor must become more important while I become less"). Thanksgiving and celebration for all that has been, and for what is still to come, can well be part of the theme that day. An informal reception can be arranged to permit the Interim Pastor and the members of the congregation to say their good-byes. Such expressions of love and warmth are good for the congregation and the departing Interim and will help assure a smooth transfer of loyalty and affection to the new pastor.

Like installed pastors, many Interim Pastors wonder what relationships, if any, they can continue with members of a congregation where they have completed their term of service. Some careful guides will counsel, "Once a pastor has departed, there should be no further relationships of any kind with members of that congregation." Most Interim Pastors would agree with this advice, and they usually find it easier to follow than do installed pastors. After all, the Interim Pastor does not have the same length of time to develop lasting relationships. If, however, the Interim Pastor remains in the same presbytery or nearby, the temptation to keep up friendships begun in an earlier assignment may be real. The key to this problem seems to be, as one pastor put it, "You do not need to cut off all relationships with your former parishioners, but you do need to develop *different* relationships, appropriate relationships." For those with questions about this matter, the Committee on Ministry should be their guide.

Reflection and Evaluation

"There is an element of mystery in ministry, and the Holy Spirit does not always act through persons in predictable ways," wrote the author of the *Pastoral Activities Index.* The quality of the spiritual life of a particular pastor is beyond measurement, and yet that may be the most important factor in the pastor's impact upon a congregation and the community. Even though much of the pastor's work deals with intangibles, there is still a great deal that can be clearly evaluated, and such a review and analysis of work done, of work not done, and of the results ought to be part of the closing days and the follow-up for every Interim.

Who is to see that such an evaluation occurs? Principally, COM is responsible for the health of the churches and ministers in the presbytery and should make sure that some kind of evaluation is part of the closure of every interim ministry. At the same time the Interim Pastor and the session also may well be involved in their own reflection and evaluation processes. In some presbyteries the session is asked to prepare a letter of evaluation of the interim experience and of the Interim Pastor. This is sent to the COM with a copy to the Interim Pastor. The Interim Pastor's self-evaluation and assessment of the congregation and of the session during the interim experience are also prepared so copies can go to COM and to the session. In addition, some COMs conduct exit interviews with every departing Interim Pastor.

Those who want to understand the pastoral evaluation process in some detail will find that the booklets in the Vocation Agency's Toward Improvement of Ministry (TIM) series are quite useful, especially the *Pastoral Activities Index,* the *Session Activities Index,* and the *Pastoral Performance Profile.* Other more concise evaluation suggestions are found in Appendix B and the bibliography of this manual.

How are such evaluations used? The results should be shared with all persons who participate in the evaluation. The Interim Pastor will grow from every such experience, learning how to do a better job next time. Individual members of the session may never again have to serve as active elders during an interim period, but even so, their remaining work on the session and all their continuing service to the congregation will be enriched by fully completing the interim tasks that are theirs. COM may possibly benefit the most from a responsible review process. This committee should provide some way to make sure that the learnings from each interim experience can be preserved in a form for subsequent use by that same committee or its successors in presbytery service. Too often an evaluation is filed away and benefits no one after its first reading.

Evaluations of some kind are essential to effective interim ministry, and probably the best process is one designed individually to suit each congregation and the particular person who serves as the Interim Pastor.

7

Special Concerns
of an Interim Pastor

The Interim Pastor's life has many significant differences from that of a settled pastor. First, often, is the problem of high mobility. One Interim Pastor has said wryly, "This is a moving experience!" The Interim in many cases must be the kind of person who either enjoys or at least can tolerate moving frequently. If the pastor has a spouse, that person also needs to be able to tolerate frequent moves. Packing and unpacking furniture and household effects every few months is an ordeal that both partners in a marriage must be able to handle comfortably before the pastor considers undertaking interim service on a long-term basis. Some experienced Interim Pastors believe it is highly advisable to have a home base to which to retreat for rest and recreation between assignments or during periods of unemployment. They suggest that this base be more or less permanent and easily accessible. Such an arrangement can be costly, however, and there are others who feel that this is not a basic necessity. They are able to manage satisfactorily not only their housing but their feelings about not having a permanent residence.

A few presbyteries and one or two synods have at times employed Interim Pastors as members of their permanent staff. Such persons are usually able to buy their own homes and settle down in one place for a number of years, since their assignments are generally within commuting distance of their permanent residence. These positions are few in number, however, and interim ministry for most pastors today is still a "moving experience."

The Interim Pastor and spouse both need to be conscious of the loneliness that may accompany frequent moves and a number of short-term assignments in widely separated places. Both will want to provide for their own emotional and personal needs and should not depend solely on each other for such support. The presbytery and the congregation ought to be alerted to this aspect of the Interim's life, and particular plans should be designed to provide personal support through individuals and groups who are sensitive and competent to give the Interim Pastor this kind of caring love. It should also be seen as the responsibility of the Interim Pastor to take some personal initiative to deal with these kinds of needs. Some synods and presbyteries have already organized cadres of Interim Pastors. This helps to alleviate the problem. Membership in the Interim Network and the Association of Presbyterian Interim Ministry Specialists (APIMS) is another effective response to some of these needs.

Life-Styles

Interim Pastors go about living and working in a wide variety of ways. Here are some examples.

A male pastor, age 58, began doing interim service after deciding to shift gears professionally. In looking toward retirement, he built a home in a wilderness area that he made his permanent base. He lived at home during the summer months, working as a wilderness guide and with government forest services. From October 1 to early May he took interim pastorates anywhere in the country.

Another male pastor, at 45, became a skilled troubleshooter. Then he and his family chose the interim route, taking eighteen-month contracts with particularly difficult, conflict-ridden congregations. In this case, he was often appointed as Interim by administrative commissions of various presbyteries. He was probably the first Interim to develop a contract calling for three months' terminal pay to cover the gaps between new interim contracts. He has had few problems finding challenging situations in which to use his skills.

Another male pastor, at 77 years of age, had completed eleven interim pastorates, most of them relatively brief—about six to eight months. He focused on maintaining the pastoral work of the congregation and did not even touch the search process. He had a very satisfying experience using his considerable personal and pastoral skills and doing a good bit of traveling. His wife enjoyed the variety and travel, too.

One pastor, single and female, with a high degree of flexibility and mobility (two important characteristics needed by a full-time Interim), soon learned how to establish quickly meaningful support relationships with the congregation and community. While building these new friendships she learned it is also important to maintain other permanent personal and therapeutic ties in order to provide an emotional and social balance during days of isolation and transition. For this minister, the Interim Pastorate was a conscious career choice made during seminary years. One of her reasons was her hope that her work as Interim Pastor would increase the church's openness to women as installed pastors.

A black pastor, recently retired from service in a congregation in a large city, was able to remain in his own home there. In his retirement he served as Interim Pastor in a strong white congregation in that city so successfully that they wanted to call him as their installed pastor. He declined the invitation, however, and continued to serve effectively as Interim Pastor in a variety of different congregations in that presbytery.

Another pastor, 55 and male, was a teacher in a metropolitan area. His interim tasks involved mostly weekend and evening work. He was called twice to work in large and demanding congregations as an Interim Pastor. He found the work challenging and exciting, enabling him to use pastoral skills that he enjoyed but did not get to use in his everyday work.

A Clergy Couple (both husband and wife ordained as Ministers of the Word) found a congregation willing to call one of them as their installed pastor. That church, however, was unable to offer any kind of call to the other partner to this marriage. By working closely with the presbytery and synod concerned, the other pastor found a very satisfying ministry in serving a series of interim assignments in congregations near the spouse's call.

Family Concerns

Any person who is seriously considering interim service should have a high tolerance for rapid changes in life and work, and, if the person is married, the spouse also should be able to enjoy (or at least accept) frequent changes in living and working conditions. Except in the most unusual cases, it would seem unwise to expect young children or adolescents to move every few months. Very

careful thought needs to be given to this matter if an Interim Pastor
has children who live at home.

An Interim Pastor's spouse can make a contribution to interim
service that is much more than just supportive. The spouse can take
a unique place in the ministry of the gospel. A genuine interest in
all kinds of people and a kindly response to them will do much to
strengthen the life of the church at this difficult time in its history.
Just being present in the congregation at worship or at social occasions is a kind of witness itself, and some will find many other ways
to share in the ministry.

On a personal level, one spouse, Betty Kent, commented about
her experience as the wife of an Interim, "You become closer to
your spouse because he is the only close person you have, but it is
lonely, especially for the wife." She also pointed out that the Interim Pastor is always very busy at first in every new situation, but
the spouse does not have nearly as much to do once the home is
settled. The spouse, therefore, needs to have some absorbing personal interests to take up in those days. Betty said, "I bake a lot—
pies, cakes, cookies—in those early days of each interim." This is
one of the reasons why settling quickly into a new home is very
important. Manses are often sadly neglected, whether in regular
use or not. Therefore, the Interim should make sure that the home
to be used will be in a move-in condition when the pastor arrives.
Betty adds, "The Interim Pastor's wife should live her life in her
own style, as though each call is permanent. She should do what any
pastor's wife would do . . . do as *she* thinks best!"

The Single Person

Does all this mean that single persons find it harder to be effective Interim Pastors? Definitely not! The single person is usually
more accustomed to making friends quickly and further, as the
pastor, has a built-in natural network of friends in the church officers, members of presbytery, and the like. In addition, the single
person usually has fewer personal possessions to move and can
sometimes make important decisions more quickly because no
other member of the family has to be consulted. In many ways, the
single person is in a position to adapt easily and quickly to the
interim style of life.

The level of stability, both personally and professionally, of any
Interim Pastor is always a matter of concern. People who are themselves in the midst of significant personal transitions may not work

very well in transitional jobs. Some divorced or divorcing persons, for example, may be traumatized temporarily by their personal experiences. Some congregations are, in a similar way, traumatized by the loss of a particular pastor. Obviously it would not be wise to call a traumatized person to a traumatized church. There are on record, nonetheless, a number of instances where recently divorced ministers have served very effectively as Interim Pastors. The key, of course, is to know the pastor well and to make a careful match to an appropriate congregation. Stability is not directly related to marital status. The single or divorced pastor can be fully as effective as the married one.

Financial Security

Because the life of the Interim Pastor is considerably different from that of the installed pastor, it is important for the Interim to plan carefully all aspects of a personal financial program. Careful negotiation with session committees and COM in developing the financial details of a contract is essential. Salary, pension, and medical benefits all need to be thoughtfully worked out. Moving expenses, both going to and returning from an interim assignment, need to be settled as part of the initial contract. Retired persons who are serving as Interim Pastors need to be particularly careful about pension and Social Security benefits. Significant savings in income tax can be effected if the right arrangements are made in each interim assignment.

Another significant concern for those involved in interim service relates to providing for one's financial needs during the possible hiatus between assignments. At this stage, only a few persons are employed by governing bodies on a full-time basis as Interim Pastors who receive a regular salary. Most Interim Pastors have to deal with the fact that they can never be sure they will have a constant income. Further, the amount an Interim Pastor is paid may vary widely from one assignment to another. The Interim must make provisions for this fact. If the Interim Pastor can build up some financial reserves, either before going into interim service or during such a ministry, many problems can be alleviated.

Stress, Mobility

Recent studies have pointed out the high incidence of stress and burnout in nearly all the helping professions. This includes the ministry, of course, and interim work is one of the more uncertain and stressful forms of ministry. The frequent moves, lack of job security, being without the more normative support systems, subjected to a constant change of doctors, dentists, and community services, and the normal aggravations related to moving can be a source of real distress. As much as any minister, and perhaps more, Interim Pastors need to pay attention to the level of stress in their lives and then make conscious efforts to deal with and reduce that stress. There are at least a dozen good books on this subject, written just for ministers, and one of the better ones is *Stress Management for Ministers* by Charles L. Rassieur. He emphasizes the importance of self-care in little ways as well as in major ways. Effective time management is one form of essential self-discipline that Interim Pastors particularly need. In addition, proper diet, exercise, and rest can help reduce the negative impact of a high-stress life-style. Above all the Interim Pastor needs to develop a personal spiritual discipline in forms that can readily be carried anywhere and practiced at any time. Personal meditation, worship, and journal writing can give any pastor a quality of character that makes life virtually burnout-proof.

For some, however, there is a better experience to report. One Interim Pastor, after describing a number of problems he had faced, added, "If the above sounds forbidding, I have overdrawn the picture. I have found that during my interimships, I lived and worked under a great deal less pressure than during my pastorates. An Interim Pastor is not responsible for the introduction and nurture of long-term policies and programs. The Interim is not as likely to be on call day and night as an installed pastor would be. Living accommodations will often be smaller and simpler than those of a manse. Consequently, the Interim will not be expected or able to do as much entertaining as an installed pastor." Clearly, for this man, part of his success in dealing with stress was his own attitude toward his life circumstances. It is wise to emphasize the positive, as a rule.

Housing

Between assignments, the Interim Pastor may be without a place to live, and it would be helpful if the Interim had some established roots (a home or family with whom to live). Otherwise, such an Interim should be willing to live without roots or established home or family ties. This may seem a rather bleak picture of the Interim Pastor's life, and a person who seriously considers this as a calling needs to take into account the possibility that all these conditions could converge at the same moment and life could be rather difficult if there are not inner resources ready to deal with such a development. Nevertheless, many pastors who have given a number of years in interim service find great joy in their work and consider it a most rewarding ministry.

Re-entry Into an Installed Pastorate

Persons who have served one or more Interim Pastorates, and who are not retired, sometimes want to return to the status of an installed pastor, for a variety of personal reasons. The spouse may be weary of frequent moving. The Interim Pastor may be equally worn out after ministering to what seems like a procession of church officers and members. Those who have come to this point generally find that return to more traditional forms of ministry is not easy. Experienced Interim Pastors have pointed out that nearly all non-parish clergy or specialized ministers have a difficult time in finding a call to a parish position. Interim Pastors are not much different. Most pastor nominating committees want a pastor with fresh experience in a pastorate. They hesitate to call specialized ministers because they fear such ministers are out of touch with the parish. Sometimes a search committee seems to fear that specialized ministers may have turned their backs on parish ministry when they entered their specialty service. Only by very careful effort is it possible to persuade most PNCs otherwise.

Another element seems to work against the Interim Pastor who wants to return to an installed position. Moving every year (or more often) gives some people the impression that a pastor is undependable or lacks staying power. People in general distrust someone who moves around a lot. While pastors who have served only one interim may not have too much difficulty in returning to an installed position, the longer a person has been in interim service, the more difficult it is to return to a conventional position as a parish pastor.

When an Interim Pastor expresses a desire to return to an installed position, all the resources of the presbytery, the synod, and the General Assembly should be made available. Relocation to a new position is seldom easy for any minister in the Presbyterian system, but diligent and careful search usually brings the desired reward. Success in such an effort means careful preparation of a new Personal Information Form, well before the search begins. Then if the regular system is used fully, and if other channels for reaching PNCs are also followed, success will come.

A number of stereotypes still work against the Interim Pastor who wants to move to a more permanent call, nevertheless, and more attention needs to be given to this problem if the interim movement is to continue to attract competent and stable pastors.

Retirement

The majority of Interim Pastors today are retired persons whose years of experience have equipped them to deal easily and comfortably with the problems of the parish, and whose maturity should give them the ability to handle division in the congregation and hostilities among members and groups. Further, retired persons generally have only one dependent moving with them, and this is easier than uprooting an entire family every six to twelve months. In addition, retired persons often have pensions or supplemental income, and this means they can accept service assignments where there is only modest remuneration.

At present well over 3,000 ministers in the Presbyterian Church (U.S.A.) are listed as honorably retired. There are many of this number whose age or health makes it impossible for them to serve in any professional capacity. Others, however, are finding interim ministry offers a very satisfying way to continue in service to the church.

In the first place, it can provide a way in which to continue a fruitful ministry without all the strains and pressures of a full-time pastorate. The ministry is a demanding calling, and forty years in it often leaves a person exhausted, whether the service has been as pastor, teacher, missionary, evangelist, or administrator or in some other position. On the other hand, the retired minister may not want to stop entirely. Interim service could be for three to six months of the year, leaving time for travel, recreation, writing, or other pursuits.

There are good retirement provisions ably administered under the pension plan, coupled with generous provision for hospitalization, so there is not as much financial pressure as there used to be for a minister to try to stay active longer. Interim supply service would serve as a dependable source of additional income, however, if needed or desired. Also, there has been increasing interest in encouraging earlier retirement. With interim service as a viable option, many ministers might choose to retire earlier.

Interim service enables a retired person to visit, serve, and live for a while in various parts of the church. Some Interims have achieved remarkable success in spending the summer in the northern parts of the church and the winter in Florida or the Gulf Coast. Such good fortune is unusual, of course, and one should not enter interim service for that reason alone.

The best way to hold off the encroachments of aging, we are told, is to remain mentally and physically active as much as possible. Nothing ages a person so much as just quitting or slowing down to a crawl. Most can maintain good health better by engaging in some productive work for the Lord. Interim service is not the only way to do this, but it is one of the better ways.

In some observations he made several years ago Edward W. Ziegler, one of the earliest Presbyterian Interim Pastors, wrote to a friend, "For some retired ministers the interimship is an answer to prayer. Thus far, it has been my privilege to serve in that capacity in two churches, one in the East and one in the Midwest. I recommend this form of ministry to any retired pastor who is reasonably healthy, loves people, is adaptable to new situations, is receptive to new ideas, still feels a tingle of excitement when confronted by problems and opportunities which so often go hand in hand, and who does not mind a bit of moving about."

8

The Growing Edge
of Interim Ministries

For more than ten years certain denominations have been experimenting with a number of carefully organized intentional approaches to a variety of kinds of interim ministries, but efforts have been focused chiefly in the interim pastorate.

Significant progress has been made both in the theory and practice of interim ministry mainly on the initiative of the Alban Institute, the Mid-Atlantic Association for Training and Consulting, and the Interim Network, as well as some advocacy and developmental programs they have spawned. The Episcopal Church, the Lutherans, the United Church of Christ, the Disciples, the American Baptists, the United Church of Canada, and a number of smaller denominations have been leaders in the expansion of this movement, but until recently the group with the largest number of pastors actually in the practice of interim ministry was probably the Presbyterians. (Presbyterians have had the largest membership of any group in the Interim Network since its inception.) The concept itself is now well established and the movement is beginning to enter a second phase, expanding into additional fields of service and influence. The developing strength of the Interim Network and the creation of the related Association of Presbyterian Interim Ministry Specialists are indications of one way this growing edge is beginning to develop.

Many presbyteries have now adopted the policy that only a few years ago was a rarity, that every church while seeking a new pastor must employ a trained interim ministry specialist, an intentional Interim. As mentioned earlier, perhaps a dozen or more presbyteries (and some synods) now employ a full-time intentional Interim Pastor who is seen as a member of the presbytery's paid staff but whose only assignment is to serve as Interim Pastor of congregations seeking an installed pastor. A few presbyteries now have two Interim Pastors on staff full-time with full salary guaranteed by the presbytery. The trend is growing, and more governing bodies (including some synods) are planning to call resident Interim Pastors.

Executive Interims

Another new development is that presbyteries and synods themselves are employing intentional interim ministry specialists as interim executives when the head of staff of the governing body retires or moves to another position. Experience seems to indicate that the dynamics of a transition in leadership in the presbytery or synod are much the same as in a congregation, with few significant differences. The Rev. Joan Mabon has recently served in several interim executive positions. She has written:

> When a governing body loses executive staff, this body . . . like any other system of relationships . . . is faced with a number of new concerns. The body as a whole needs to say good-bye to the departing executive, to honor that person's gifts . . . to deal with anxiety about maintaining present mission objectives. . . . An Interim Executive can offer a governing body the time to manage the awesome tasks at hand as well as the opportunity to celebrate and learn from the past before they are pushed too soon into the future.

Ms. Mabon also points out:

> An Interim Executive can offer the governing body's churches a model for using the interim period fruitfully. As more and more presbyteries and synods begin to encourage congregations to seek interim leadership, that encouragement is far more persuasive if the governing body itself can demonstrate commitment to this concept. When a governing body shows that it, too, is . . . deeply concerned for the relationships that are a part of its very body, then its intention for strong interim ministry is believable.

Other forms of specialized ministry throughout the church are also beginning to tap into the interim theory, learnings, and practical experience that have proved so valuable to congregations over the past decade. Synods, presbyteries, and all COMs would be wise to begin now to consider these additional ways in which interim ministry specialists can be employed to advance the mission of the church in their areas. The Rev. Lawrence D. Spencer, a specialized minister in Houston, has pointed out several ways in which interim ministry can expand. Some of his suggestions are in the following paragraphs.

Interim Educators

Directors of Christian Education, serving as Interim Educators in a congregation or on a governing body staff, can be of major assistance while a search process is under way for a permanent staff person, particularly if the Interim Educator understands the special significance of the interim time in a congregation or governing body's life and is willing to make a commitment to that specific opportunity to guide change and development (and perhaps reconciliation) in that time. Such persons can be equally valuable to congregations, presbyteries, synods, and General Assembly ministry units. College and seminary professors and higher education administrators can also serve in special roles to meet unique needs of the institution if they learn interim theory and practice and if the institutions themselves are open to experiment with this form of leadership for managing change.

Interim Chaplains

Hospitals, nursing homes, sanitariums, rehabilitation centers, prisons, halfway houses, and many other kinds of caregiving organizations are learning to make effective use of a chaplain's services. The chaplain with a firm grasp of the interim minister's special task and mission can be of significant service to any of these places or programs when guided change, sensitive maintenance, or reconciliation are needed in special circumstances and for limited periods of time.

Interim Administrators

Executive or associate executive administrators (with general or specialized job descriptions) can serve in any of the denomination's mission or ministry units and agencies, the various councils of churches and other ecumenical alliances, or even in church-related or church-approved secular or government service programs. Presbyteries and their COMs will find that recognizing the validity of these forms of ministry, including interim specialists in these fields, will greatly strengthen the church and its mission.

Other Specialized Interim Ministries

Even a brief study of The Acts of the Apostles, especially the opening chapters, will remind the reader of just how innovative and energetic the early church leaders were in their own response to the ministry and mission Christ had given to them. The Gospels, too, reflect a band of disciples ready to invent new forms, to reinterpret traditional ways, to follow their Lord wherever his ministry took them or sent them. Our contemporary church must learn to be as open and creative, tolerant and discerning, yet patient and caring as were those first of Jesus' followers. Interim Pastors are teaching the church a new way of looking at its life, especially in times of transition. Seldom has the church faced any more volatile time than in these present years. The church's present strength and its future growth are, as always, in the hands of its own people, supported by Jesus Christ, the Foundation and Chief Cornerstone. A wider, more informed, more flexible use of interim ministry in all kinds of new fields is one way now, not only to sustain the kingdom of God on earth but to bring to it both reconciliation and new growth.

Appendix A
Suggested Interim Pastor Contract

The following contract between the session of _____ Church and the Rev. _____ is for the purpose of providing interim pastoral services to _____ Church.

Elements:

The Rev. _____ will be designated Interim Pastor of _____ Church. *(Any statement relating to the ordination of the pastor and/or transfer to the presbytery if not a member would be inserted here.)*

The Interim Pastor

Will/will not become (is) a member of _____ presbytery.

Will/will not serve as moderator of the session.

Will/will not serve as head of staff.

Will/will not assist the presbytery consultant in the conduct of the mission study. If so, in what way?

Will/will not assist in preparation of the Church Information Form. If so, how?

The Interim Pastor will be responsible for providing pastoral duties as indicated on the following position description, which shall include provision for evaluation. *(Suggestions for writing a position description are found in* Guidelines for a Session Personnel Committee, *3rd ed., of the* Toward Improvement of Ministry *series of booklets listed in the bibliography. The* Pastoral Activities Index *from the same series has a helpful list of ministerial tasks that will also assist in the preparation of such a position description. The following are examples only.)*

Lead worship and preach _____ Sundays per month.

Provide for a leader of worship on Sundays not present.

Do pastoral calling on sick and shut-ins as time permits.

Officiate at weddings and funerals as requested.

Plan and moderate session and congregational meetings.

Work with boards and committees to assist them in carrying out their assigned tasks.

Train newly elected officers in conjunction with staff and selected members.

Perform other administrative duties as requested: i.e., work with church secretary in preparing bulletins, newsletters, etc., exercise general oversight of church facilities, and represent the church in dealing with outside organizations.

Note: Duties as spelled out should be consistent with the full- or part-time status of the candidate. It may be useful to add: The normal work week will be _____ hours per day and _____ days per week. *Another form some pastors are using is:* The normal work week will be 10 [or 12 or 13] modules per week. *(A module is one morning or an afternoon or an evening.)*

Goals for this ministry shall be *(examples follow)*:

Maintenance of a healthy congregational life.

Continuity of leadership.

Development of short-range goals identified in the goal-setting process of the church.

Preparation of the congregation for the arrival of a new pastor.

Assessment of the congregation's needs to call an installed pastor.

During the length of the agreement, Rev. _____ will be accountable to the presbytery through the COM. At the end of the contract, _____ Church agrees to provide a performance review.

It is understood that should the Interim Pastor have any serious differences or difficulties with any former pastor(s) of this congregation, the matter will be referred to presbytery's COM.

It is understood that the Rev. _____ has agreed not to be involved in any way with the Pastor Nominating Committee, except to see that they make adequate reports. Any suggestions the Interim Pastor has are to be submitted to the COM. *Or* the Rev. _____ will serve the Pastor Nominating Committee in the following ways *(describe).*

It is understood that the Rev. _____ has agreed not to be a candidate for the pastoral office of _____ Church and in every way will seek to prepare the way for the coming of an installed pastor.

This agreement is for a period of _____ months *(not more than twelve,* Book of Order *G-14.0513b)* from the date below. This agreement may be terminated by the session upon 30 days' written notice. The Interim Pastor may terminate the agreement with 30 days' written notice and forfeiture of any payment beyond the 30-day period. This agreement may be extended in _____ month periods.

Terms: The Interim Pastor is employed on a full-time *(part-time = 1/2,*

2/3, etc.) basis, serving approximately _____ hours per week (*or modules per week*), and will be compensated for interim pastoral services as follows:

Base salary:	$_____	
Housing allowance:	$_____	*(Any statement concerning manse or any special housing arrangements shall be included here.)*
Full pension:	$_____	
Auto allowance:	$_____	*(Include any statement involving travel on the job. The amount for car allowance should equal mileage plus depreciation.)*
Medical care:	$_____	*(Retired persons are not covered for Major Medical under the pension plan, so some provision may be needed here.* * *Provision for deductible for nonretired pastors may also be a consideration.)*
Moving costs:	$_____	*(Costs to and from the field can be specified in terms of the total actual cost, or a maximum allowable dollar amount can be set.)*
Vacation:		To be earned at the rate of 1 week per quarter and used each quarter *(or accumulated as agreed on).*
Study leave:		Two weeks prorated annually *(including financial assistance consistent with the congregation's provision for the last installed pastor or according to presbytery's standards).*

Any released time provisions for special commitments and any other conditions of service shall be listed.

Full salary and allowances shall be paid the Interim Pastor as necessary, not to exceed a period of three months from the start-up date of the incoming pastor. This does not include such vacation and study leave as may be due at the time of termination.

---

*Interested persons should write their own pension office for full details: The Board of Pensions, 341 Ponce de Leon Avenue, NE, Atlanta, GA 30308 or The Board of Pensions, 1834 Arch Street, Philadelphia, PA 19103.

Appendix B
Evaluation Form

Evaluation of_____

Interim Pastor of_____

From _____ 19____ to _____ 19____

Please rate each of the activities listed below. *Leave blank* any activity you had no opportunity to observe.

	Poor				Excellent
	1	2	3	4	5
1. Leading worship and sacraments	—	—	—	—	—
2. Preaching	—	—	—	—	—
3. Implementing agreed-upon goals	—	—	—	—	—
4. Spiritual development of members	—	—	—	—	—
5. Congregational home visits	—	—	—	—	—
6. Hospital and emergency visits	—	—	—	—	—
7. Promoting congregational fellowship	—	—	—	—	—
8. Counseling services	—	—	—	—	—
9. Evangelism (introducing people to Christ)	—	—	—	—	—
10. Planning congregational life and mission	—	—	—	—	—
11. Managing conflict	—	—	—	—	—
12. Development of educational program	—	—	—	—	—
13. Teaching responsibilities	—	—	—	—	—
14. Mission in the local community	—	—	—	—	—
15. Congregational communication	—	—	—	—	—
16. Administrative leadership	—	—	—	—	—
17. Stewardship and commitment education	—	—	—	—	—
18. Financial and property management	—	—	—	—	—
19. Evaluation of program and employed staff	—	—	—	—	—

20. Responsibilities with presbytery, synod,
    GA   — — — — —
21. Work with youth and children   — — — — —
22. Implementation of goals agreed upon   — — — — —
23. Healing of grief over the past   — — — — —
24. Clarification of congregational identity   — — — — —

What was the most helpful part of this interim?

Additional comments or suggestions:

Appendix C
Information for Interim Pastor Roster

Name: _____ Date: ____

Present Address: _____ (Phone)____

Permanent Address *(if different)*: _____ (Phone)____

Available for assignment beginning (date):_____

Interim work experience *(give churches and addresses; if you have no interim experience, list your most recent parish experience)*:

Have you had any formal interim training? List what, when, and where.

What specialized interests and experiences do you have?

Why are you interested in interim ministry?

Limitations on assignments *(geographic, part-time, etc.)*:

Other specific preferences *(type and size of church, climate or location, length of assignment, etc.)*:

Financial needs:

List three persons who can evaluate your work and suitability for interim ministry *(include at least one executive presbyter and one Committee on Ministry chairperson)*:

Use an additional page for these data if necessary.

Appendix D
The Process of Change

In *New Hope for Congregations,* Loren B. Mead describes Project Test Pattern's work in four case studies of parishes that were provided with outside "parish development adviser/consultants" in order to assist in the change process. While these consultants were not Interim Pastors, much of their work is related to the Interim's tasks. From those experiences, Mead isolated the following four learnings about congregations:

1. Congregations can change.
2. Congregations have a history that influences the change process.
3. Congregations are unique, and the model must be adapted for each situation.
4. The ways in which people relate to each other, information is communicated, and decisions made have great power in shaping a congregation.

He also isolated five learnings about the process of change in congregations:

1. Third-party consultation can increase the rate of effectiveness of change in a congregation.
2. Covenant/contract relationships between parish and consultants must be carefully spelled out.
3. The pastor's own commitment to change will be a key to the extent to which a congregation will change.
4. Consultants, pastors, and congregations need support systems to help them handle anxieties related to change and uncertainty.
5. We can learn much from failures if we are open to examining them.

Finally, Mead makes the point that renewal is not a program; it is a process. As such, it is properly part of the ongoing life of the congregation and is not delimited by any single experience or effort.

Elisa L. DesPortes elaborated upon Mead's work in her book *Congrega-*

tions in Change. In it she described the change patterns in five other parishes that were included in Project Test Pattern. After isolating what could be learned from each case study, she enumerated seven concepts regarding congregations in change that have general applicability. They are:

1. People have an enormous commitment and investment in their congregation.

2. The parish's history has a tremendous influence on its present life.

3. The geographic situation of a church is an important influence in its life.

4. The tension between mission and maintenance can be a source of growth for the parish.

5. There are a variety of models for consultative help that can be effective.

6. Information about a parish has an important influence upon the congregation.

7. Parish norms are difficult to change.

Appendix E
Procedures and Policy—One Presbytery's Program

At the interim time, Congregational Development and COM, acting for Presbytery, support churches in two specific ways, through a Vacancy Team and through Interim Leadership.

Congregational Development and COM support the congregation, its boards and committees, through its work with the Interim Pastor. Congregational Development and COM relate to the Interim Pastor in these ways:

1. Assist in contracting.
2. Provide orientation meeting with description of the parish situation—its strengths, weaknesses, significant issues, and tasks.
3. Communicate in writing to session the specific expectations of Interim Pastor, session, and congregation during vacancy.
4. Appoint presbytery representative to be present at first worship service to introduce Interim Pastor, interpret context, and symbolize liaison with presbytery.
5. Provide helpful start-up and termination forms.
6. Appoint team to conduct periodic review of Interim Pastor.
7. Support Interim Pastor in training to upgrade skills and knowledge for interim work.
8. Evaluate Interim Pastor's work with session before new pastor is installed.

Through its Vacancy Teams, Congregational Development and COM support is focused specifically on the search for a new pastor and related work. Since this work can affect the whole congregation, Vacancy Teams relate to the Interim Pastor in the following ways:

1. Share pertinent information from the previous pastor's termination interview with the Interim Pastor.
2. Share congregational goal information with the Interim Pastor.

3. Keep Interim Pastor advised of the search status and tentative timetable.

4. Refer to the Interim Pastor any problems that may need pastoral care and issues that session or its committee should address.

5. Deal with problems related to term of Interim Pastor.

6. Provide input and participation in celebration of the new pastoral relationship.

Interim Pastors relate to congregation, to Vacancy Teams, and to Congregational Development and COM in some of the following ways:

1. Follow as closely as possible short-term goals chosen by the congregation or session.

2. Articulate and, when necessary, review personal goals for the interim work.

3. Attain minimum requirements for interim leader to work and seek to upgrade skills in this area.

4. Meet with Congregational Development and COM Team for goal/work/review.

5. Work closely with Vacancy Team in any relationship to pastor search committees; refer committee members to team for any questions.

6. Keep "hands off" the search committee except to provide personal reflection on how accurately the view of the church is pictured in the Church Information Form; advise, if appropriate, how a searching candidate might interpret the Church Information Form.

7. Avoid giving candidates' names directly to search committee.

8. Communicate to Vacancy Team any session action that will affect the search.

9. Provide a concise evaluation of interim period to be shared with Vacancy Team in the termination review.

Appendix F
Steps Toward an Interim Pastor

Time
Line

_____ 1. Formal request by the session.

_____ 2. Presbytery COM meets with the session to outline steps and authorizes session to proceed.

_____ 3. Session Personnel Committee
3.1 Develops position description
3.11 What do you want your Interim to do?
3.12 Use Toward Improvement of Ministry handbooks
3.2 Determines salary guidelines
3.3 Determines term of service, i.e., "The term of employment shall be *(3, 6, 9, 12 months or specific date)*, with the privilege for negotiation of adjustments in the contract by the session and the Interim Pastor."

_____ 4. Session
4.1 Approves Personnel Committee plan
4.2 Notifies COM for critique

_____ 5. COM and session, coordinated by the Session Personnel Committee, seek the person through
5.1 Personal contacts
5.2 Church Vocations Unit
5.3 Interim cadre
5.4 Suggestions from COM and presbytery or synod executive

_____ 6. Session (or its representatives)
6.1 Screens interim candidates
6.2 Interviews them
6.3 Hears them preach and lead worship

        6.4 Decides on the Interim it wants

        6.5 Requests approval of presbytery through COM

———— 7. COM recommends approval of presbytery

———— 8. Presbytery gives approval

———— 9. Person starts interim pastorate

(The Equal Employment Opportunity guidelines of your presbytery should be followed throughout this process.)

Appendix G
"Rehearsing Our Story"*

Interim Pastors need to help a congregation come to terms with its history. In so doing, the congregation begins to gain a sense of its identity. Rehearsing our story tells of the myths that formed us and that continue to give us direction.

A key figure in our story is Loren Mead. As director of the Alban Institute in Washington, D.C., he has been instrumental in helping to determine both the need for and the unique nature of the interim ministry.

Interims have been going on for a long time. Two hundred years ago somebody filled in while a church waited for a new pastor. But the story of recognized and intentional interim ministry is rather recent. It begins in 1970, when it came to Loren Mead that perhaps the principles of Organizational Development might be applied to the work of a church in interim, thereby broadening the scope of what it means to be an Interim. Despite the interesting results of that experiment, nothing much happened. There was not enough energy or interest to keep the momentum going until others began to question what to do with capable, skilled retired clergy who had much to offer. This concern developed into a ministry-at-large program for the Baptist Church. Around this time others became interested in interim work: Ray Welles, an Episcopal priest in California, who did his doctoral work in interim ministry and eventually wrote a book, *Between the No Longer and the Not Yet;* Cynthia Brandt, who wrote her master's thesis in this area and began doing interim ministry in 1973; and Tom Tupper, on the national staff of the United Church of Christ, who shared the dream and pursued it with the Alban Institute.

In 1975, realizing that it was time to begin gathering data and technology on the nature of interim ministry, the Alban Institute organized a Symposium on Interim Work in St. Louis, sponsored by the Patton Foun-

---

*By Roy M. Oswald, abridged from the Report of the First Annual Interim Network Conference, June 1981.

dation. They invited people who were involved in interim ministry and placement to spend three days telling about what they do (the Kübler-Ross approach), in order to explore what happens and what is done. Alan Gripe, a Presbyterian from the national level, attended to see if interim was worthwhile and discovered a new kind of career for ministry with real possibilities. From the St. Louis learnings, Loren Mead wrote the first guide for Interim Pastors, and Ralph Macy produced a fine article "The Interim Pastor."

The year 1976 saw the MATC (Mid-Atlantic Association for Training and Consulting) program begin to work with vacancy consultants. This program (Interim Pastors/Consultants Training Program) is now training mainly Interim Pastors.

Other training programs were provided in 1978 and 1979 through the Alban Institute for the American Lutheran Church and the Presbyterian Synods of Mid-America and Synod of Lakes and Prairies. We began to work on the idea of forming an indigenous organization, and an initial group of planners gathered at St. Maur's in Indianapolis in 1979. The Interim Network began. The next year a steering committee gathered to design and produce the First Annual Interim Conference in Madison, Wisconsin, in 1981.

A couple of very important lessons have been learned over the last ten years. First (and most important) is the issue of being open to a call from the congregation you are serving as an Interim. This act will break the back of interim ministry, because other pastors will begin to view this as the way to get a church. We need to continually monitor ourselves. Perhaps there should be an annual pledge of allegiance: "I will not become a candidate for the congregation I am serving as an Interim."

A second learning is that we need to begin involving lay people in the Network and begin dealing with issues faced by spouses and families of Interim Pastors.

And then there are observations and dreams. As a "budding specialty" we are probably the least supported of all ministers in what we do and need a network to come to for support. There are not a lot of people who can really understand what we are about because they have not experienced the life of an Interim Pastor. A vital part of our support should come from judicatories, who need to be challenged constantly to upgrade the interim work in their churches. As a network we need to press the systems toward excellence.

We are small at this time, and the job is great. There are many others not currently involved in the Network who are doing interim ministry. We need to encourage them to join and work with us to upgrade the quality of ministry throughout the entire church by having top-notch Interims. The more Interims we have who do good, the more interim work there will be to do.

People are calling more and more for "trained" Interims. Our dream should include the monitoring and improvement of all training programs. Every middle judicatory executive should have at least two competent Interim Pastors. This would be a gold mine for any executive.

Annotated Bibliography

General Resources

Alban Institute, 4125 Nebraska Avenue NW, Washington, DC 20016. Phone: 800 457-2674.

A multidenominational agency that shares practical resources and ideas about congregations across denominational, hierarchical, and clergy-lay lines. Works for congregations in four ways: research, publishing (many publications are listed in the bibliography), consulting, and training. Publishes quarterly journal, *Action Information,* available to persons on the mailing list (back issues also available). The Alban Institute provides discounts to "judicatory partners" when materials for clergy and congregations are ordered in quantities of ten or more.

Association of Presbyterian Interim Ministry Specialists (APIMS), P.O. Box 106, Linden, NJ 07036.

This organization has established standards for certification and credentialing of Interim Pastors. Write for information. Works closely with Interim Network.

Interim Network, 5885 Robert Oliver Place, Columbia, MD 21045. Phone: 301 730-6806.

An ecumenical organization of Interim Pastors and their spouses, interim consultants and governing body staff. The Network provides a forum wherein members from a variety of denominations have opportunity for support and dialogue on the development of sound policies, practices, and ethical standards for interim ministry together with frequent training events for professional development.

Mid-Atlantic Association for Training and Consulting (MATC), 1500 Massachusetts Avenue NW, Suite 325, Washington, DC 20005. Phone: 202 223-0585.

Increasing numbers of judicatories are using MATC's Clergy in Transition Institute as part of the education and training strategy for newly assigned clergy and those in changing congregations. The Institute deals with transition, power, and conflict in the congregation, and "reflection-feedback planning." Brochure available. MATC annually conducts training programs for Interim Pastors and Vacancy Consultants. These are some of the best such courses available. Write or telephone that office for details.

Minister's Life Resources, 3100 West Lake Street, Minneapolis, MN 55416.
Several series of resource materials—cassette tapes, pamphlets, books—dealing with a variety of problems of concern to pastors, such as the minister's finances, personal and professional growth, the minister's own marriage and family, and personal support groups. Brochure available.

Church Development and Change

DesPortes, Elisa L. *Congregations in Change.* New York: Seabury Press, 1973. A Project Test Pattern book on parish development. Six studies on congregational renewal, a companion to Loren Mead's *New Hope.*

Jones, Ezra Earl, and Robert L. Wilson. *What's Ahead for Old First Church?* New York: Harper & Row, 1974.

Mabon, Joan. "Interim Pastors and Interim Executives, Is It Any Different?" *Presbyterian Outlook,* September 8–15, 1986, p. 6.

Mead, Loren B. *Critical Moment of Ministry: A Change of Pastors.* This is a book for pastors and lay persons who lead congregations through changes in leadership. It tells how differently clergy and lay leaders experience such critical moments, what processes need attention, and what all this means for the future of the congregation. Washington, D.C.: Alban Institute, 1986.

———. *New Hope for Congregations.* Stories of four churches with reflections on the dynamics of congregational life and the process of change. Washington, D.C.: Alban Institute, 1972.

Schaller, Lyle E. *Survival Tactics in the Parish.* Nashville: Abingdon Press, 1977. Follows a fictional pastor through nine years at a church to illustrate concrete, proven tactics to restructure and restrengthen the parish.

Smith, Donald P. *Congregations Alive.* Philadelphia: Westminster Press, 1981. Practical suggestions for bringing your church to life through partnership in ministry.

Walrath, Douglas Alan. *Leading Churches Through Change.* Nashville: Abingdon Press, 1979. Six case studies.

Clergy Spouses

Cavicchia, Karen D. *Pastor's Spouse: Person or Puppet?* A seminar report presented to the faculty of Guidance on Counseling, Southwest Missouri State University, December, 1978. Available from John Calvin Union Presbytery, 1835 South Stewart Street, Springfield, MO 65804.

Clinebell, Howard and Charlotte. *The Intimate Marriage.* New York: Harper & Row, 1970. This is one of the better guides for strengthening the marriage relationship.

Rediger, G. Lloyd. *But I Don't Have a Recipe for Manna.* Madison, Wis.: Wisconsin Council of Churches, 1976. A selection of articles and a workbook designed to help wives of clergymen to understand themselves and their roles. Some sections may be helpful to husbands of clergywomen too.

Sparks, James. "Criticism and the Minister's Wife." Chapter 7 of *Potshots at the Preacher.* Nashville: Abingdon Press, 1977.

Truman, Ruth. *Underground Manual for Ministers' Wives.* Nashville: Abingdon Press, 1974. A lively and insightful discussion of what it means to be a minister's wife, the pains, the plagues, the satisfactions and the joys; this work has some very practical advice for beginners and some new ideas for old hands.

Conflict Resolution and Role Definition

Bridston, Keith R., et al. *Casebook on Church and Society.* Nashville: Abingdon Press, 1974. Provides insights into many current areas of conflict in church and society, including internal church conflicts and changing attitudes on issues.

Glasse, James D. *Putting It Together in the Parish.* Nashville: Abingdon Press, 1972. A practical do-it-yourself book, this volume includes several useful chapters about managing change in parish life and one, chapter 9, on the topic "Learning to Fight like Christians in the Church."

Harris, John C. *Stress, Power, and Ministry.* Issues of stress and power in clergy and laity's lives together. Focus on personhood of clergy and their relationships with lay people and church systems. Washington, D.C.: Alban Institute, 1978.

Harris, John C., and Celia A. Hahn. *A Study Guide for Stress, Power, and Ministry.* Outlines a seven-week course to help clergy and laity examine issues in Harris's book as they exist in their life together. Washington, D.C.: Alban Institute, 1979.

Leas, Speed B. *A Lay Person's Guide to Conflict Management.* Washington, D.C.: Alban Institute, 1979.

————. *A Study of Involuntary Terminations in Some Presbyterian, Episcopalian, and United Church of Christ Congregations.* Washington, D.C.: Alban Institute, 1980.

Leas, Speed B., and Paul Kittlaus. *Church Fights: Managing Conflict in the Local Church.* Philadelphia: Westminster Press, 1973.

Lewis, Douglass. *Resolving Church Conflicts.* San Francisco: Harper & Row, 1981. A case book for congregations.

Mead, Loren. *Clergy Evaluation: Who Owns It?* Monograph. Washington, D.C.: Alban Institute, 1974.

————. *Evaluation: Of, By, For, and To the Clergy.* A paper on evaluation, exploring the person, the task, the performance, and the context. Washington, D.C.: Alban Institute, 1975.

Mickey, Paul A., and Robert L. Wilson. *Conflict and Resolution: A Case-Study Approach to Handling Parish Situations.* Nashville: Abingdon Press, 1973.

Miller, John M. *The Contentious Community: Constructive Conflict in the Church.* Philadelphia: Westminster Press, 1978. On creating unity in the midst of the church's natural diversity.

Rassieur, Charles L. *Stress Management for Ministers.* Philadelphia: Westminster Press, 1982.

Schaller, Lyle. *The Change Agent: The Strategy of Innovative Leadership.* Nashville: Abingdon Press, 1972.

————. *The Multiple Staff and the Larger Church.* Nashville: Abingdon Press, 1979.

Smith, Donald P. *Clergy in the Cross-Fire: Coping with Role Conflicts in the Ministry.* Philadelphia: Westminster Press, 1973.

Swan, Allan H. "Planning for Crisis" 1975. Doctoral dissertation on file, San Francisco Theological Seminary Library, San Anselmo, CA 94960.

Vocation Agency. Toward Improvement of Ministry series. Materials include: *Pastoral Activities Index* (2nd ed.), *Pastoral Performance Profile* (2nd ed.), *Planning for Ministry, Guidelines for a Session Personnel Committee* (3rd ed.), and *Session Activities Index.* Order from Vocation Agency, Room 420, Interchurch Center, 475 Riverside Drive, New York, NY 10115.

Interim Pastorates

Interim Network. *The In-Between Times: Interim Network Newsletter.* Published every three months. Write: Interim Network, 5885 Robert Oliver Place, Columbia, MD 21045.

Macy, Ralph. *The Interim Pastor.* Theoretical and practical paper clarifying the unique contribution of the Interim Pastor. Washington, D.C.: Alban Institute, 1978.

Small Church

Blunk, Henry A. *Smaller Church Mission Study Guide.* Philadelphia: Geneva Press, 1978.

Carroll, Jackson W., ed. *Small Churches Are Beautiful.* New York: Harper & Row, 1978.

Dudley, Carl S. *Making the Small Church Effective.* Nashville: Abingdon Press, 1978.

———. *Unique Dynamics of the Small Church.* A look at small, economically marginal churches, examining their special dynamics, life-styles, and sources of strength and morale. Washington, D.C.: Alban Institute, 1977.

Gravely, Herbert C., Jr., and Spencer R. Quick. *The Use of Organizational Development Consultations/Small Mission Congregations.* Project Test Pattern, June 11, 1973. Washington, D.C.: Alban Institute, 1973.

Madsen, Paul O. *The Small Church—Valid, Vital, Victorious.* Valley Forge, Pa.: Judson Press, 1975.

Mathieson, Moira. *The Shepherds of the Delectable Mountains: A Study of the Washington County Mission Program.* Case study of three small churches in Appalachia where laity were trained to take over clergy roles. Washington, D.C.: Alban Institute, 1979.

The Small Church 1975. Special report of the Synod of Lakes and Prairies, Office of Communication. 8012 Cedar Avenue, South, Bloomington, MN 55420.

Transitions: Churches Without Pastors

Alban Institute. *Prime Time for Renewal: Judicatory Packet.* Filmstrip and cassette for denominational staff persons to use with vacant pulpit churches. Also includes *The Developmental Tasks of the Parish in Search of a Pastor* (Mead) and *The Minister Is Leaving* (Hahn).

———. *Prime Time for Renewal: Parish Packet.* Resources for the search committee. Includes *Dear Calling Committee Member* (Ramsey) and *On the Calling and Care of Pastors* (Kirk), 12 copies each; 1 copy each of *The Minister Is Leaving* (Hahn), *Prime Time for Renewal* (Yon), *Do You Know the Way to San Jose?* (Bullock); and two posters.

Kirk, Richard J. *On the Calling and Care of Pastors.* Kirk examines four critical "opportunity points" in pastor-parish relationships. Helpful advice for the lay board whose pastor has just resigned. Washington, D.C.: Alban Institute, 1973.

Mead, Loren B. *Changing Pastoral Leadership.* Resources available to "bishops" in vacancy work. Washington, D.C.: Alban Institute, 1976.

———. *The Developmental Tasks of the Parish in Search of a Pastor.* Helping congregations work through necessary tasks as they search for a new pastor. For staff persons and persons in churches. Washington, D.C.· Alban Institute, 1977.

Sackmann, Robert C. *A Sensitive Presence* 1980. A helpful guide to a person representing the COM in work with a pastor nominating committee.

Contact: Dr. Robert C. Sackmann, 1514 East Third Street, Bloomington, IN 47401.

Transitions: The Minister Changing Positions

Bolles, Richard N. *What Color Is Your Parachute?* Berkeley, Calif.: Ten Speed Press, 1987. (Updated annually.)

Bullock, A. Richard. *Do You Know the Way to San Jose? One Pastor's Search for a Job.* How one clergyman managed his transition from one position to another. Washington, D.C.: Alban Institute, 1975.

Fletcher, John C. *Religious Authenticity in the Clergy.* Three crises through which a clergyman becomes authenticated as minister of a congregation. Washington, D.C.: Alban Institute, 1975.

Harris, John C. *The Minister Looks for a Job.* How to take an active stance when you look for work as minister of a local church. Washington, D.C.: Alban Institute, 1975.

Kemper, Robert G. *Beginning a New Pastorate.* Nashville: Abingdon Press, 1978.

Oswald, Roy M. *New Beginnings: Pastorate Start-up Workbook.* A three-ring notebook with 80 pages of designs to help clergy as individuals or groups perform the task of transition to a new pastorate. Washington, D.C.: Alban Institute, 1978.